COME TO THE PARTY

CELEBRATE Jesus

LeRoy Lawson

STANDARD
PUBLISHING
Cincinnati, Ohio

The Standard Publishing Company, Cincinnati, Ohio
A division of the Standex International Corporation
©1994 by The Standard Publishing Company
All rights reserved
Printed in the United States of America

01 00 99 98 97 96 95 94   5 4 3 2 1

Library of Congress Cataloging in Publication data:

Lawson, E. LeRoy, 1938–
    Come to the party! : celebrate Jesus / LeRoy Lawson.
       p. cm.
    Includes bibliographical references.
    ISBN 0-7847-0144-X
    1. Joy—Religious aspects—Christianity. 2. Worship.
3. Christian Life—1960– 4. Lawson, E. LeRoy, 1938–   . I. Title.
II. Title: Celebrate Jesus.
BV4647.J68L385   1994
248.4—dc20   93-28842
                                                  CIP

Contents

Introduction

Let's Celebrate

Nehemiah 8:1-12

In my files is an undated page ripped from the letters to the editor section of *Christianity Today*. A somber believer from Hampton, Virginia, scolds: "The Christian life is essentially serious. This is a vale of tears. Humor has no place in the pulpit or the Sunday school." Worship in this gentleman's church must be pretty grim business. He intends his letter as a call to repentance from frivolity and a return to holy sobriety. His bile would escalate should anyone suggest, as this book will, that he cease his whimpering over how hard his life, how heavy his burden, and begin to celebrate!

He could be blessed, if he would, by this little Zen poem:

Gone my fine old hopes.
Dry my dreaming.
But still iris blue each spring.[1]

In the driest season there is reason to smile.

He could profit also from an introduction to Theodore Roosevelt. My high school principal was a fan of the former President, whom he often quoted. Roosevelt's battle with—and victory over—childhood asthma inspired me, a fellow wheezer. This exuberant super-charged President exuded energy, as if forever making up for his sickly start. Everything delighted him. When he was facing the convention that would nominate him in his own

5

right (after filling out the assassinated President McKinley's unfinished term), Ambassador Jean Jules Jusserand of France remarked of him, "The President is in his best mood. He is always in his best mood."[2]

What a tribute to the man. Not a bad goal, either, this perpetual best-moodedness. Certainly beats the Virginia gentleman's gloom.

Moods are not something we're born with, nor something with which we are permanently saddled. Nobody forces them on us; we cultivate them. They sprout out of our largest convictions, the ones about God and life and what it means to be God's person. The Virginia gentleman worships a stern God, more sovereign than savior, wielding a forbidding scepter over a battle-scarred world. For him life in general and the Christian life in particular are under attack; only the siege mentality is appropriate. Any hint of frippery is out of order.

For Roosevelt the overcomer, God is good and life is delightful.

Humanity is mostly one or the other, pouty or grateful. Some, it must be admitted, can't decide which they are, so their moods swing wildly depending on . . . well, depending on a lot of things—the weather, the economy, the current state of their relationships or finances or fancies. They are like the children Paul speaks of in Ephesians 4, "tossed back and forth by the waves, and blown here and there by every wind of teaching and by the cunning and craftiness of men in their deceitful scheming." They just don't know what's what and can't decide whether to pout or give thanks. So they waffle.

This author has chosen thankfulness, because his life has been filled with delight, and the appropriate expression is celebration. Life isn't exactly a cup of tea; it's more like a cool drink of spring water to a perspiring field hand. To a man who has known both the perspiration and the refreshing spring, life is worth the living. Celebration comes easy.

It also enjoys God's sanction, as we learn in a most unlikely source, the Old Testament book of Nehemiah. Skip the familiar story of Nehemiah's dramatic return to Judah to lead his compatriots in rebuilding the Jerusalem wall. The odds against completing the project are heavy, but God and the people win. The whole story is a good read, but our interest is in chapters 8–12, where another voice takes up the narrative to speak of the rekindling of the spiritual fire of Nehemiah's formerly defeated people. In these chapters, the priest Ezra and his assistants read the long-forgotten Law of Moses to the people, who repent of their long years in spiritual barrenness. When the priests call them to an obedient hearing of the Word of the Lord, the nation vows before God to adopt it anew as the foundation of national faith and culture.

Pay close attention to 8:9-12, a surprising text. Three times in these few verses Nehemiah, Ezra, and the priests instruct the people in words that still startle us. We are unaccustomed to marrying sanctity and partying, but it is holiness and gloom that don't belong together. When we modern believers think of Old Testament worship, we are more likely to recall something like Leviticus 23:27:

The tenth day of this seventh month is the Day of Atonement. Hold a sacred assembly and *deny yourselves,* and present an offering made to the Lord by fire.

This is more like it: sacred assembly, self-denial, sacrifice.

Yet, when the Feast of Tabernacles instructions were given in Deuteronomy 16:13-15, self-denial hardly was the dominant note:

Celebrate the Feast of Tabernacles for seven days after you have gathered the produce of your threshing floor and your winepress. *Be joyful* at your Feast—you, your sons and daughters, your menservants and maidservants, and the

Levites, the aliens, the fatherless and the widows who live in your towns. For seven days celebrate the Feast to the Lord your God at the place the Lord will choose. For the *Lord your God will bless you* in all your harvest and in all the work of your hands, and *your joy will be complete.*

With this reminder of God's love of celebration, we are now ready to return to Ezra and the reading of the Law from break of day to noon:

They read from the law of God, making it clear and giving the meaning so that the people could understand what was being read.

This is verse 8. Then comes the astonishing ninth verse:

This day is sacred to the Lord your God. *Do not mourn or weep.*

Mourning and weeping are exactly what they *had* been doing. They had fallen under conviction. The sacred words burned in their hearts; they had neglected their holy duties. They were guilty before God. They deeply regretted their disdain for the things of God. Shouldn't they be weeping? Not according to Nehemiah:

Go and enjoy choice food and sweet drinks, and send some to those who have nothing prepared. This day is sacred to our Lord. Do not grieve, for *the joy of the Lord is your strength.*

Then the Levites joined in to calm the people:

Be still, for this is a sacred day. Do not grieve.

The people did as they were told:

Then all the people went away to eat and drink, to send portions of food and to celebrate with great joy, because now they understood the words that had been made known to them.

What a surprise. *This day is sacred to the Lord your God.* How does one behave in the presence of the Lord, on his holy day? With penitence, sackcloth, and ashes? With the rigidly enforced, nearly absolute inactivity of a Puritan Sunday? No: *Go and enjoy choice food and sweet drinks,* and share what you have with others. Celebrate. Be joyful, for in "the joy of the Lord is your strength!"

Celebration: Worship and Sacred Rite

When our Mesa church worship leaders were developing the new Saturday evening service, one of the first problems to be solved was what to call it. "Saturday Night Alive" was suggested but quickly dismissed; too many other churches had already borrowed and modified the famous television program's name. We wanted to be original, we thought.

We ended up being unoriginal but quite accurate. "Saturday Night Celebration," it's called.

Celebrating is what we do on Sunday morning as well. *Celebration* is increasingly in vogue as the name for a church's worship service. The term signals more than a mere semantic change. It signifies a sharpened yet more inclusive view of worship. The attention is on God, and the attitude is joyful thanksgiving. Believers are taking time and pains to let God know how they feel about him and the life they enjoy because of him. While the elements of meditation and petition and study have been retained, the mood has switched from solemnity to joyful celebration.

Come, let us sing for joy to the Lord;
let us shout aloud to the Rock of our salvation.
Let us come before him with thanksgiving
and extol him with music and song (Psalm 95:1, 2).

Sing to the Lord a new song;
sing to the Lord, all the earth.
Sing to the Lord, praise his name;
proclaim his salvation day after day.
Declare his glory among the nations,
his marvelous deeds among all peoples (Psalm 96:1-3).

Note that the celebrants don't consider themselves the audience in this celebration. Their singing is to the Lord, who revels in their song and dance and festive spirit as a father enjoys watching his children enjoying themselves. Worship is awareness of God, gratitude beyond vocabulary, thanksgiving that takes the whole body to express itself, a reaching upward from our depths to touch God in his reaching down, a grateful trust that in spite of all contrary outward appearances God is working for good.

Worship is celebration is thanksgiving is praise. So we

Enter his gates with thanksgiving
and his courts with praise;
[we] give thanks to him and praise his name (Psalm 100:4).

Worship is gratefully remembering God's goodness, love, wonderful deeds, and righteousness.

Praise the Lord.
Give thanks to the Lord, for he is good;
his love endures forever (Psalm 106:1).

Let them give thanks to the Lord
for his unfailing love
and his wonderful deeds for men.
Let them sacrifice thank offerings
and tell of his works with songs of joy (Psalm 107:21, 22).

In that day you will say:
"Give thanks to the Lord, call on his name;

make known among the nations what he has done,
and proclaim that his name is exalted" (Isaiah 12:4).

They will celebrate your abundant goodness
and joyfully sing of your righteousness (Psalm 145:7).

Even in the midst of national desolation, believers in God are encouraged to rejoice, as Jeremiah exhorted the people of Israel:

This is what the Lord says: "You say about this place, 'It is a desolate waste, without men or animals.' Yet in the towns of Judah and the streets of Jerusalem that are deserted, inhabited by neither men or animals, there will be heard once more the sounds of joy and gladness, the voices of bride and bridegroom, and the voices of those who bring thank offerings to the house of the Lord, saying, 'Give thanks to the Lord Almighty, for the Lord is good; his love endures forever.' For I will restore the fortunes of the land as they were before," says the Lord (Jeremiah 33:10, 11).

There you have it. Rejoicing, singing, eating, drinking, dancing, sharing, thank-offerings, celebrating as at a wedding feast. Such are the mood and the manner of worship.

Celebration: Partying

Throughout this book *celebration* will often mean *partying,* but a further word is in order for the young reader. It wasn't so when I was in school, but today's young people insist that the word now has a very specific meaning. *Partying* is *drinking,* pure and simple. To go partying is to drink it up, usually to excess.

While Biblical celebration includes eating and drinking, doing either to excess is not condoned. Unlike certain religions, the Christian faith encourages sanity and sobriety, qualities not in the least opposed to festivity and celebration. We are to love the Lord with all our minds and are never encouraged to leave them behind when approaching God, as certain mystery and spiritist religions do.

Christian celebration is best illustrated in Jesus' simple story of the prodigal son's return to his long-waiting father. The occasion called for partying.

> Bring the fattened calf and kill it. Let's have a feast and celebrate. For this son of mine was dead and is alive again; he was lost and is found.' So they began to celebrate (Luke 15:23, 24).

There was no other way to express the father's relief, gratitude, and sheer joy in having his son with him again.

In recent rereadings of the story, however, I have been wondering. Is it possible that there had been too little partying in this home before? When the younger son broke away, partying was all he wanted to do. Was he starved for festivity in his life? And when the elder brother protested the party being thrown for the returned prodigal, his complaint suggests that he hadn't had much fun in his life, either: "Look! All these years I've been slaving for you and never disobeyed your orders. Yet you never gave me even a young goat so I could celebrate with my friends."

Celebration is the worship of God, but it is more. It is exulting in the presence of one's friends and loved ones. It is, in the old fashioned sense of the word, partying.

Celebration: An Attitude Embracing Life, an Honoring of the Honorable

Celebration is even more. It is a socially approved way to pay honor to someone to whom honor is due. The party often has a focus. If the focus is God, we call it worship. If the focus is another person, one we are *celebrating,* we speak of the *celebrated* guest at the party. If the person is regularly so honored, is recognized as special by many people over time, we append the word to the person: he or she is a *celebrity.*

12

Thus in Christian circles we meet regularly to celebrate in honor of God; the name we wear honors Christ. Our sermons and stories laud Biblical heroes like Moses, David, Ruth, Naomi, Mary, Paul, Peter, Barnabas, Mary, and Martha. Lessons on Christian history laud giants like Augustine, Aquinas, Luther, Calvin, Wesley, Knox, Campbell, Moody, and contemporaries like King, Graham, Mother Teresa.

The habit of celebration reinforces the positive, appreciative spirit that gave it birth. Banished is the curled lip, the sophisticated sneer, the pouty complaint. When the author Walter Pater died, Oscar Wilde, fancying himself clever, scoffed, "Was he ever alive?"[3] In one question Wilde managed to smear Pater, diminish life, and define himself. When Wilde later died, few mourned. Withholding honor from others, he was in the end denied honor himself. The celebration of life demonstrates grateful satisfaction with God's gifts of breath and body and thought and movement and community and meaning.

So we celebrate, in gratitude.

One last word. I have been speaking of attitude, mood, thanksgiving, choice—of what's *in* you rather than what's *out* there. The assumption has been that the impetus for celebration is not in the environment but in the celebrant.

The delightful curmudgeon Andy Rooney, grumping happily at the absurdities of contemporary civilization, puts the pouter's creed into perspective. "Life is bad for you," he says. We are bombarded, he complains, with "bad news about what's good for us."

> How often does a day go by that you don't hear about something else you eat or do or don't do or wear or own that's bad for your health? At least once a week they announce another item on our diet that's suspected of causing cancer. If it doesn't cause cancer, it brings on heart attacks.

The fact of the matter is, life is bad for you. For one thing, living brings on age, and we know how debilitating age can be. It's something everyone should avoid.

I wouldn't be surprised if the government started making us wear little labels that said, "Caution: the surgeon general has determined that living is dangerous to your health."[4]

Actually, living *is* dangerous.
• The food you eat
• the air you breathe (especially in major cities)
• the water you drink
• the house you live in (think of the chemicals)
• the green things that grow around you (if you are prone to allergic reactions)
• the people you associate with (many criminal and deviant types are among them)
• the roads you travel (you know the accident statistics)
• the programs you watch (such harmful ideas)
• the government that takes your last dollar in taxes
• the church you attend (which sometimes preaches as truth what isn't true)

It is impossible to be alive and not in danger. You'd better watch out.

But you had better not watch out too much. You have to live, you know.

What then should you do? Would you live? Would you thrive? Remember the two-fold task of Nehemiah and Ezra: to rebuild Jerusalem's wall and to revive Jerusalem's people. The first the people accomplished by the sweat of their brows, the second by their return to worship. They gave thanks, they praised, they partied. The enemies had not vanished, the obstacles were multiple, the danger ever present. But they were alive again.

Since danger always is present, you might just as well give thanks and celebrate.

Christian celebration is the theme here, and celebration is about the music and dancing and clapping and singing and the overflowing of joy in persons touched by the grace of God. These chapters only barely introduce the subject, but a quick glance at the contents will reveal the opportunities for celebrating when you

- experience the miracle of birth
- cheer a bride and groom into their new union
- answer the Lord's call to ministry
- meet the physical needs of hungry people
- win others to Christ as Lord and Savior
- return home when your immature rebellion is over
- care enough to give your very best
- praise God whether others like it or not
- are reconciled to the Lord after you've really blown it
- stand forever in the presence of the Lord
- seriously decide to rejoice always
- encourage others toward their success
- faithfully commune at the Lord's table

This author, who cannot imagine a more joyful life than the one he has found in Christ's service, hopes these studies help you develop your own rich life of celebration. Paul is right. You really can "rejoice in the Lord." *Always.*

---

[1]Quoted by Steven Rockefeller in "Facing the World," Bill Moyers, *A World of Ideas.* New York, et al: Doubleday, 1990, p. 173.

[2]*A Sense of History, Writings from the Pages of American Heritage.* Ed Byron Dobell. Boston: Houghton Mifflin, 1985, p. 550.

[3]Richard Ellman, *Oscar Wilde.* New York: Vintage Books, division of Random House, 1987, p. 52.

[4]Andrew A. Rooney, *The Most of Andy Rooney.* New York: Galahad Books, 1986, p. 324.

Chapter 1

When Luke Was Born
in the City of Mesa...

Luke 2:1-20

I'll never be able to think of Jesus' birth the same way again, not after being there when Luke was born. *Luke Aaron Denton,* I mean, not the Luke the Gospel is according to.

It seems that every time I read the Christmas story— at least once a year and sometimes more often, depending on whether I run across it in my devotions or am cross-referencing a text for a sermon—I spot something I have overlooked before. For that matter, we seldom read any Scripture the same way twice. We approach each reading from a little different angle or as a somewhat different person. The Bible remains the same, but we don't.

My reading of the Christmas story changed dramatically for me when Luke was born. The birth of Jesus, my birth, everybody's birth became different, a living symbol of God's love. There in the labor/delivery room I remembered the God who so loved the world that he sent a baby to save it. And I wondered again, as I had when Luke's mother was born, what unexpected grace this new baby was delivering from God.

It's not that I didn't know how babies get here. I am a grandfather, after all. You can't live as long as I have and not know, even if you weren't brought up on a farm (and I became well acquainted with the ways of the barnyard in my childhood). Even a non-farm kid knows these things now. There's television, of course, and magazines that nowadays publish unsparing, clinically accurate pictures. So I knew what would happen, but knowing and being there aren't the same. And I was there.

The invitation had been offered before, for Nick's appearing twenty months earlier, but my flight from England couldn't be hurried, and Nick couldn't wait. So his grandmother enjoyed the privilege of being there, and I had to hear about things secondhand. This time the grandmother stayed home to take care of Nick and his older brother Kyle. It was not an easy day for her, with Nick's being less than two and Kyle just three-and-a-half—a handful for a grandmother, even a doting one. She loves them, but I couldn't help suspecting, although she never mentioned it, that she'd rather have been helping Luke to arrive. She didn't say so, because she knew how much the grandfather had been looking forward to being there.

He'd been wanting to be there for twenty-nine years, ever since Luke's mother was born. But in those days doctors seemed to believe fathers were dangerous to the mother and the new baby and the whole birthing operation. So I was banished to the fathers' waiting room, a sterile, cold, impersonal holding tank for superfluous persons. "We'll tell you when the time comes. Don't worry about a thing. Just be patient. These things take time. She's going to do just fine." There we were, another expectant father and I, two haggard looking exiles from the action, whiling away the hours while the excitement took place elsewhere. He paced and smoked. I just paced, until even pacing seemed superfluous. Then I slept.

It seemed unjust. I had been there for the conception, and had tried to offer a little encouragement during the gestation with its attending morning sickness and mood swings and multiplying uncomfortablenesses. At the end of the nine months I drove her to the hospital where I was permitted to mop her brow and hold her hand and massage her back during the mounting terrors of labor, but as the grand climax approached, nurses scurried and the obstetrician was summoned and the father was banished.

Only later, when calmness returned, was I told of the result and, after the scrubbing and weighing and recording of pertinent data, allowed to see our child for myself and visit the pale but triumphant mother.

Thus I missed the big moment, a denial I was still loudly lamenting a score and nine years later. I expected to go to my grave in this state of deprivation. Even though in recent years physicians had discovered that the presence of fathers may not be lethal after all, they received their revelation some years after I was a candidate for fatherhood.

And who would ever invite the grandfather?

That one of my daughters would do so I had never dared dream. That her husband would agree seemed beyond imagining, this being such an intimate moment for the two of them. But she did, and he did, and I was there, grappling with a turbulence of emotions I had never experienced before. Wanting to shout my gladness and pray my gratitude and dance my ecstasy, I succumbed to quietness instead. Later, holding five-minute-old Luke in my hand, I called his grandmother to share the good news. "Everybody's fine," I assured her. "Only one person cried." Silence answered. "Okay, two."

Why did they cry, these two happy, proud, excited third-time grandparents? The mother, Kim, smiled, a little weak from the ordeal, but grinning nonetheless. The baby's father, Royce, beamed. Another son. Three boys, all healthy, bright, and energetic. At once we could discern Luke had sturdy, strong arms and neck; we could tell by the tilt of his head he wouldn't be a passive one. But his grandfather, who was there, felt unusually subdued, smiling but choking up when talking to the grandmother, who couldn't answer for a while, either. A wonderful moment, a moment of wonderment. It happens all the time all over the earth, this birth giving, but for us that day, it seemed, well, miraculous, as if we were holding something from beyond mere human coupling and reproducing, from somewhere beyond egg and sperm and multiplying cells. A moment ago Luke was a fetus floating in his mother's womb, fully formed and human, but still being supplied by her love and warmth and fluids. To us he appeared a mere distention of her abdomen, a source of exquisite pain; to her he was inward joy, occasional pangs, and a constant reminder of the mystery of life and the goodness of God.

And now I was holding him. A baby. A person. A gift from God.

After the miracle, the grandfather stayed on his cloud all week, that strange conflux of emotions still holding sway. Amazement, profound gratitude, and an irresistible impulse to tell anyone, everyone he could corner, about his experience. Not just about the baby, but about his experience at the birthing. Sometimes his friends were rude. They interrupted. Other grandparents were the worst. They had stories of their own. He became impatient with their tales. Theirs were, well, just stories. His narrative was different. He had had an experience unique in the chronicles of humankind.

Here, in the city of Mesa, Luke was born. Heaven came down and wrought a miracle. And I was there.

I almost said, "I was present at the creation." The allusion is not to Genesis but to the title of a well-known book of memoirs by Dean Acheson, President Truman's Secretary of State. His title referred to the rebuilding of Europe in the aftermath of World War II. One of the architects of a new world, his creative mind gave birth to the helpful Truman Doctrine and the Marshall Plan.

Acheson's title is appropriate here. To Dean Acheson and Harry Truman and other world leaders had been handed the task of lifting Europe and Japan from the ashes of military and atomic destruction. The glories that once had been the Empire of the Sun and the Civilization of the West had been eclipsed; the world was groaning in travail. Humanity could not return to what had been; something new had to take its place. Some new hope had to be born.

Some new hope. That explains the sudden loss of speech to the normally loquacious grandfather that day in the Mesa hospital room. He was holding hope in his arms. Time was running out on the old man. He's not ready for a rest home, not yet, but his years are taking their toll. Things he once could do he now can do no more. The evidence is conclusive: he will go to his grave with his "To Do" list unfinished. The mark he wanted to make will be dimmer than he intended. The world will not be saved in his generation.

For Luke, though—ah, the possibilities. He has come to a planet in need of a fix. Too many exploiters have ravaged its continents; marauders and mercenaries and men of war have nearly finished it off. What the world needs now is someone willing to restore it, someone who will love it enough to purify its air, clear its muddied waters, restore its ravaged forests, protect its endangered species (including the one we belong to), rescue its hurting humans, repair its fractured families, and lead nations to wage war no more. Here, in my arms, is one who can do more and greater things than his grandfather has ever attempted, one who must succeed where his grandfather has failed. There isn't much time left. My generation has failed; his might not. There's hope. He's hope.

Before the doctor left the labor/delivery room, he surprised me by a simple, beautiful gesture. Dr. Chatterjee is Indian, having come to America from his homeland many years earlier. He is young no longer. I suspected, though I didn't ask, that he might be nearly as old as the grandfather. I took to the man immediately. He exuded brusque competence; he was clearly in command and his demeanor commanded respect. But that isn't what appealed to me. My father's heart could sense he cared about my daughter. That mattered. He was a tender, gentle man, this no-nonsense physician. What counted equally was his obvious joy in his work, his uncynical respect for new life. It was what he did at the end that moved me most.

Having tended to the mother's physical needs, he turned once more to the baby. Holding him in his hands at arms' length, he bowed his head to Luke. Was it a religious act or just a salute to the newborn, the gesture of a humble man in the presence of mystery? Was he like Simeon, who blessed Joseph and Mary and praised God for the baby whom he called "God's salvation"? I didn't know, but my heart bowed with him, and was warmed.

When Jesus was born in Bethlehem to Mary, his was a unique and wonderful birth. But now I wonder—was his birth more wonderful than Luke's in Mesa? Or was it unique and wonderful as is the birth of every baby whom loving parents and watching angels attend? Of Jesus' specialness we have no doubt. The Bible tells us so. But doesn't the same Bible tell us that Luke's birth in Mesa is also special to God and that this baby also is unique, unlike any other anywhere else?

Unique loses its meaning—or regains it—when applied to human personality. "One," it means. Special one. The only one like this one. But it can also connote "individual as all other human beings are individual, one of a kind." Jesus' birth is celebrated because Jesus, son of Mary, son of Holy Spirit, "son" of Joseph, is God's unique gift to humanity, and he has never given another gift like him.

At the risk of sounding too much the grandfather, may I assure you that Luke Aaron Denton is also God's gift to humanity? So was Nicholas Emmanuel Denton before him, and Kyle Christian Denton before him. I can never look at the birth of Jesus the same again, having been present at the birthing of my grandson. On the other hand, I can never be casual about the birth of my grandson or any child any more, having learned of the birth of my savior in Bethlehem.

The angels sang the night Jesus was born, their music filling the firmament with praise. Were they singing because they, as I, were present at the birthing of one unlike any other ever born? Were they celebrating their Sovereign's wondrous gift to earth? Once you have been present at the birth of a loved one, you feel compelled to join the angels in celebrating the advent of God's Son on earth. It isn't any wonder, is it, that for all centuries since the first one, believers in Jesus have been festive at Christmas? Heaven kicked off the music and merry-making with angelic singing. God's unique Son has been born.

What a party God orchestrated. Who else would have thought to include on the invitation list shepherds, who come quickly to see for themselves, their costumes a little grimy and smelling of sheep? Or for that matter, wise men from the East, learned and wealthy and accustomed to honor, now in their joy stooping to offer praise to Mary's Son? Saintly old Simeon hasn't been forgotten, either, able now to die in peace because he has seen God's salvation in the flesh. Neither has ancient Anna, temple-bound for so many years but now telling anyone who'll listen that here is, at long last, the One who will redeem Jerusalem. What can we say of Mary's inexpressible joy or Joseph's wonderful bewilderment? It is in every way a splendid party, and it is only the beginning of Jesus' celebrated life, a life so deliciously unpredictable only God could have written the script. Max Lucado calls the amazing script God's "sacred delight."

What is sacred delight? It is God doing what gods would be doing only in your wildest dreams—wearing diapers, riding donkeys, washing feet, dozing in storms. Delight is the day they accused God of having too much fun, attending too many parties, and spending too much time with the Happy Hour crowd.[1]

And when God is delighted, you can hear the angels sing all over the heavens.

We didn't hear the angels singing when Luke was born; we took their place. The grandparents sang the praises of his mother and father, of the attentive and sympathetic nurses, of the good physician, and of the Giver of every good and perfect gift, including this one.

We also meditated on some of life's biggest questions, or at least the grandfather did. Why was this baby born? That is only a less egocentric form of the puzzle that disturbs most of us from time to time: Why was I born? In Jesus' case, the Scriptures tell us. His very name does: He is Jesus (which means Savior, or God saves) the Christ (the Anointed One or Messiah), nicknamed "Lamb of God" (who takes away the sins of the world). He is Son of God (revealing all of God we can comprehend) and Son of Man (revealing all of humankind we can become). He was born, in other words, to do us good, to convey God's saving love to us.

Thus Jesus. But why me? Why you?

I already confessed that when Luke was born, his grandfather's hopes were transferred to him. There's still a big world out there, and most of it needs saving. Jesus has done the essential work; now Luke and Nick and Kyle and you and I can help him complete the project. When we became Christians, the Bible says, we put on Christ and now Christ lives in us. Since his purpose toward humanity hasn't changed any, he has made us fellow laborers with him in his great rescue operation. We were born and reborn to live for others, to do them good.

This understanding of our purpose for living isn't peculiar to the Bible. You and I aren't the only ones who raise the question, and we aren't the only ones who come to this same satisfactory answer. I was really impressed when I read what Jason Gaes, the twelve-year-old cancer victim who wrote *My Book For Kids With Cansur*, found through his ordeal. When assigned to write a school paper on the question, "Why are we born?" he found the writing difficult. He couldn't think of anything for a long time. Then he gradually began to make sense of his own life and illness, and wrote,

> I think God made us each born for a different reason. He doesn't want us to do the same things so that's why he makes us all so different. If God gives you a great voice maybe he wants you to sing. Or else if God wants you to be a farmer he might give you to a family that lives on a farm so you get used to the animals and your not afraid of them. And maybe if God makes you grow to be 7 feet tall maybe he wants you to play for the Lakers or the Celtics.

Jason had a little friend Kim who died of cancer when she was only six. He wondered why God let her be born in the first place, if that was all the longer she was going to live. His mother explained that though Kim was only six, she changed people's lives. Then he realized he could do the same.

> I used to wonder why did God pick on me and give me cansur. Maybe it was because he wanted me to be a dr. who takes care of kids with cansur so when they say "Dr. Jason, sometimes I get so scared I'm going to die" or "you don't know how weird it is to be the only bald kid in your whole school" I can say "Oh yes I do. When I was a little boy I had cansur too. And look at all my hair now. Someday your hair will grow back too."[2]

To be a cancer victim no longer seemed so terrible, if only he could use his ordeal to give hope to someone else.

Jason has discovered the key to celebrating life. When a baby is born, we are captivated by the newborn as baby, with a baby's intrinsic beauty and charm and value. A baby has only to be, and we are delighted. But have you noticed we never stop there, with what simply

25

is? We immediately dream of what will be. Our thoughts move from the baby to the adult the baby will one day become, and we imagine the joy the adult will bring to others. We dream of his becoming a president, a star athlete, a scholar, a doctor, a scientist—always a person who contributes something to the good of others. She'll be a concert pianist, a movie star, a mathematical genius, a good mother, a businesswoman. Others will take note of her accomplishments, her contributions to social well-being.

So young Jason found in himself what we dream of on behalf of newborn babies, that he could celebrate life in the midst of his struggles with cancer because he was now gifted to help someone else. His search for meaning was over; he found peace and could put to rest the disturbing questions his cancer forced on him.

Remember my grandson Luke? (How long do you expect a grandfather to stay on another subject when he has grandkids to boast of?) Do you know what I like best about him? I honestly can't tell you, because I don't know him very well yet. I can describe the way he cries, varying distinctly in pitch and volume and sense of urgency depending on what need he wishes to communicate. Or I can detail his daily routine and how, just when we think he's settled into a predictable schedule, he unsettles us. Or I can tell you of his efficient digestive system (which takes in at one end and copiously gives out at the other) or of his physical features.

Hmmm, what do I like best about him? I guess I have to confess that what I like best about him is that he is, in a real sense, mine. We are, indeed, relatives, related by birth. We belong to each other, through the kind offices of his parents. Because of that, for as long as we both shall live, when he has a birthday, I'll celebrate. I'll celebrate *him*. I'll hope through him and pray he'll be a blessing, so that years later, even after he has died, people will remember him as we remember Jesus—and want to celebrate him.

This chapter appears to be about Jesus and my grandson Luke. I hope you have taken it personally, though, because all along I've been writing about you, especially about two often overlooked facts. The first is your own intrinsic worth. When you were a baby like Jesus, like Luke, you were also a unique person of intrinsic, immeasurable value. At what point in your growing up did you lose that value? As far as God is concerned, you never did. You have it still. Your value doesn't lie in what you have accomplished, what you have earned and saved, or what you think of yourself. It is God-given and, as far as God is concerned, permanent.

The second is that, having begun as a person of worth to God, you have an opportunity to increase your value to other human beings. In the beginning you were a gift of God to someone, inducing hope and bringing out the best in those who loved you. When did you lose that power? Didn't Jesus teach that we must become like children again if we hope to enter the kingdom? The kingdom of God exists wherever God reigns supreme. Wherever God is in charge, his subjects (you and I) are bearers of hope and love.

You are unique. There is no other quite like you. No one else has your particular opportunities to do the good you can do. You, like Jesus who was born in Bethlehem and Luke who was born in Mesa, are a gift of God, a blessing from on high.

I hope that after you are gone, whenever people remember you, they will celebrate the memory.

---

[1]*The Applause of Heaven*. Dallas, et al: Word Publishing, 1990, pp. 9, 10.

[2]Jason Gaes, twelve-year-old cancer victim, *My Book for Kids with Cansur*. Cited in *The Meaning of Life*, by David Friend and the editors of Life. A Little, Brown book.

Chapter 2

When Jesus Attends a Wedding

John 2:1-11

John says he wrote his Gospel, especially the parts about the miracles, "that you may believe that Jesus is the Christ, the Son of God, and that by believing you may have life in his name" (John 20:31). The book contains several "miraculous signs" such as transforming water into wine, healing a lifelong invalid, feeding five thousand men (and who knows how many women and children) on two small fish and five barley loaves, giving sight to a blind man, and bringing his friend Lazarus back to life. Because of miracles like these, John reports, people put their faith in Jesus.

What served to encourage faith then often acts as an obstacle to faith now. We cut our intellectual teeth on the scientific method. We "know" that nature is governed by laws that can't be broken. When a man is dead, you can't call him back to life. If a baby is born blind, when he is an adult you can't put a little mud on his eyelids, order him to wash in a certain pool of water, and expect the eyeballs suddenly to start functioning. This isn't how nature works. And you can't mutter some kind of hocus-pocus to make water taste like vintage wine.

So we struggle with the miracles, treating them as proof all right, but proof of the naivete of the people of Jesus' day rather than as proof of his divinity. We doubt in part because so many religious charlatans of our own day have made outrageous claims, only to be proved frauds in the end.

In the case of the wedding feast miracle, at least Jesus' mother believed in him, although there's no reason for us to think she expected what she got. She probably just turned to him as her eldest son (and the leader of the band of disciples) to do something to help, since he and his friends had eaten and drunk their share of the refreshments.

What happened was undoubtedly a surprise to her. John hints that it astonished his disciples, for he concludes the story, "This, the first of his miraculous signs, Jesus performed in Cana in Galilee. He thus revealed his glory, and his disciples put their faith in him." They had already believed enough to accept the call to become his disciples, but transforming water to wine seemed proof positive that they had chosen rightly.

There are several remarkable elements in this story that bear looking into. The first is that—

Jesus Is at a Party

His presence shatters our stereotype of the always serious, super-conscientious, intense Son of God. What's he doing at a party? Some scholars have pushed their speculation to an extreme, proposing that Jesus himself was the bridegroom, even though the text specifically says he was a guest. Northrup Frye says:

> It has been noticed that the behavior of Jesus at this wedding is difficult to account for except on the assumption that he was the bridegroom and consequently he and his mother were responsible for the party.[1]

Frye isn't arguing that Jesus was actually married but that John has taken some biographical kernel and mythologized it, treating it as a type of "Christ's second coming as the Bridegroom." Professor Frye goes too far. Doesn't it seem much more reasonable that Jesus, who attracted large crowds by the magnetism of his personality and teaching, would be a welcome guest at some friend's wedding? Perhaps the friend was a relative, which would explain Mary's personal involvement. Is it too difficult to imagine the Blessed Mary as someone's Blessed *Aunt* Mary?

Maybe I'm reading the passage too simply, but I have the honor to be a pastor, the most privileged of all callings. Because a pastor represents Christ to his flock, and because Christians seek the presence and blessing of God at all the critical moments of their lives, a pastor is a welcome guest (no, a welcome family member) at births, deaths, serious illnesses, weddings, crises, celebrations, and holidays. Whenever life is intensified, the pastor's presence is sought. When the pastor not only represents Christ but is like him in his quiet trust in God, his vivacious love of people, and his readiness with a word of blessing or comfort, he is sought.

Seldom is life more intense than at a wedding. Very often by the time the bride and groom stand before the minister to say their "I do's" to one another, they aren't so certain they do. Tempers flare, differences are magnified, mothers are barking orders and fathers are hiding. And they all turn to the minister to restore order and keep the peace.

Weddings have always been important in our culture, especially among society's elite. Sometimes they seem more for show than for solemn vowing. In 1980 I saved the lead article of the wedding section of the June 29 *Arizona Republic*. Lisa Hyman married Steve Bandler with the help of eight attendants apiece and a production the writer said was "no more elaborate than a Cecil B. DeMille epic." Since she had been a young girl Lisa had dreamed of being wed at the exclusive Arizona Biltmore Resort Hotel. She even reserved the hotel two months before her year-long engagement was announced. "The setting was an orgy for the senses," including thirty-five bunches of lavender cushion pompons and seventy-five dozen California stocks framing the platform and gazebo.

The party in Cana was not so extravagant, but it was a costly affair nonetheless. Jewish families saved for years so that when the time came they could offer all their friends and neighbors the feast of a lifetime. The festivities sometimes lasted a week or more.

When Joy and I were married, we didn't party for a week, but we did our best to make the wedding ceremony and reception memorable. What we remember best, however, has little to do with our planning. The preacher was late and the photographer was later. You remember such things. You also remember the children in the wedding party, doing their unpredictable best to liven the party. We had a ringbearer and two flower girls—my two little nieces, who were then as now very outgoing. As the preacher intoned his admonitions for the bride and groom, they busily waved to family and friends in the congregation. When I married one of those flower girls in Sacramento in 1992, in the middle of the ceremony I stepped aside and waved at the people, explaining afterward that I had waited thirty-two years to get even!

There's no way I am going to even the score with the ringbearer. The little boy (now measuring well over six feet tall) of about four was placed beside the best man to keep him in line. In the middle of the ceremony, little Jon reached up, pulled on Curt's jacket, and not too quietly announced, "I gotta go potty." Curt said, "Hold it, kid, hold it." He didn't. We have no pictures of the ringbearer; he had to be taken home to change his clothes.

Ours was a good wedding for this parson, because it taught me never to panic when things go wrong. Joy and I have retold the story of the flower girls and the ring bearer ever since; we never recount the things that went right.

Nor do you hear us complaining about the money we spent, even though we were both broke in those days. It was too important an event for us to be cheap. Undoubtedly some grinch at the Cana wedding was mumbling in the background that it was a waste of good time and money to throw such a costly affair. The money would be better used helping the bride and groom set up housekeeping. He makes a certain amount of sense, but he'll be overruled. In a life as tedious and grim as what befalls most of the human race, a wedding is a rare opportunity to forget for a while, to laugh and sing and dance and have a taste of what life can be at its best, if only for a day or a week. It's restorative play. Whoever said "all work and no play makes Jack a dull boy" told the truth.

It is no wonder, then, that Jesus was there, affirming life, congratulating the bride and groom, appreciating the people, even replenishing the stock of wine so the gaiety wouldn't have to end too soon.

I'm treating this first sign with more respect than perhaps I once did, after reading Ari Goldman's account of David and Maria Hefner's wedding in St. Patrick's Cathedral. It was a wedding that almost didn't happen.

The reason they wanted to be married in St. Patrick's after they had already been married two and a half years earlier, and the reason they almost couldn't have the ceremony there, were the same. David had AIDS.

Before he ever met Maria he had been involved in a six-month homosexual relationship for which he would pay dearly later. Meeting and falling in love with Maria Ribeiro changed his life-style forever. They were married at City Hall in 1984; only thirty months later David learned of his fatal illness. He deteriorated rapidly, soon too weak and helpless to work. Maria quit her job to care for him. When he was hospitalized, she slept on a cot in his hospital room.

David had a lot of time to think of ways to show his gratitude for Maria's love. He knew his Catholic wife had always wanted a religious wedding ceremony in her "dream church," St. Patrick's. She said it reminded her of the church in her little home town in Mexico.

David called and was given an appointment to see an associate pastor. They went together to see him. They wanted only a small wedding, they told him, with four guests and someone to sing Ave Maria. They explained David's health problem and requested a small stool or chair to be kept handy, in case he couldn't stand.

The priest agreed to everything and they set the time and day.

Thus it was left. They departed, reflecting on the commitment they would reaffirm before God, the one they had already made to "love, cherish and honor" each other "in sickness and in health."

Two days later the priest called to tell them he couldn't celebrate their wedding. "I'm sorry, David," the priest said this time. "You have a transmittable disease and we would be putting the church at risk to have you here."

"But sir, it is transmittable only through sexual relations. In fact, the only person at risk by my going to the church is myself. I am extremely susceptible to infection."

The priest expressed his regrets, but was firm.

After Goldman's article detailing the Hefner's plight appeared on the front page of the *New York Times'* Metropolitan News section, Cardinal O'Connor reversed the decision of Father John Clermont, who had been merely following the orders of his superior, Monsignor James Rigney, rector of St. Patrick's. David and Maria renewed their wedding vows at St. Patrick's on February 14, 1987. Valentine's Day. Cardinal O'Connor was there. Three months later, David died.[2]

Goldman's account hit me hard for several reasons: 1) In recent years, there has been a dramatic increase in the number of members of my church who have requested that I "remarry" them. In most instances, they are making up for the first time when they eloped, or simply stood before a justice of the peace. Now that they know the Lord, they want to do it right, to repeat their vows in "his church" before a real minister.

2) Many of the persons I marry got off to as rocky a start in life as David did. The difficulties persons have in

leaving a homosexual or a profligate heterosexual life-
style are well known. That David succeeded is notewor-
thy in itself. That Maria took the risk to marry him and
then proved so faithful in her love is even more so.
There are several Davids and Marias in my church.

3) The church did not refuse to remarry David and
Maria because they were of mixed faith or for any doctri-
nal reasons, but because of fear of AIDS. Admittedly,
this took place fairly early in the epidemic, when many
of us were reacting irrationally. But I couldn't help wondering how many decisions I have made over the years
based on my personal fears rather than on God's will.

4) The clergy of St. Patrick's had every right to determine who could or could not be married there, of course,
but the refusal forced me to think again about my role
as a Christian minister. What exactly is it? Do I serve
God or the state when I perform weddings? Did my ordi-
nation to preach include the right to say who could or
who couldn't marry and when? I had to think about
some couples I had refused, and why. I know very few
conscientious ministers who do not wrestle with these
questions. Perhaps their very struggle is evidence of how
seriously they take their calling, and marriage, and God.

5) The biggest reason I couldn't get the Hefner's story
out of my mind, however, had to do with their burning
desire for a totally unnecessary ritual. They were already married, after all. Why wasn't that good enough?
What made David want to endure the pain and exhaustion of this church wedding? What had kept Maria
dreaming for so many years of standing at St. Patrick's
altar? Isn't it the same thing that made Jesus a glad participant in the wedding celebration in Cana? When a
man and a woman kneel before the Lord to ask his blessing on their marriage, when they make those incredible
promises (for better, for worse; for richer, for poorer; in
sickness, in health) to one another in "his house," when
they invite their nearest and dearest to be their witnesses in this solemn occasion, they are acknowledging a

third participant in their union and a spiritual dimension to their coupling. To get city hall's approval isn't good enough; they want God's.

When you believe you are acting in accordance with God's will, wending through life's major passageways with his blessing, you feel like celebrating. Standing before a justice of the peace does not suffice; you want your friends and loved ones there, and you want "there" to be special. Then you can celebrate.

He Is on a Schedule

Even as Jesus joins in the celebration of the wedding in Cana, however, he remains aware of his higher purpose. He seems to be following a timetable unknown to his mother. "Dear woman, why do you involve me? My time has not yet come." Time for what? Time to tip his hand in public, time to launch his ministry. The timing is not strictly in his control. He is being guided by God's unseen hand. What he does and when it does it are up to his Father. Later, when his brothers urge him to go to Judea to gain publicity for his ministry, he puts them off. "The right time for me has not yet come" (John 7:6).

On several occasions in John's Gospel, John stresses Jesus' (and John's) time-consciousness:

7:30 "At this they tried to seize him, but no one laid a hand on him, because his time had not yet come."

8:20 "Yet no one seized him, because his time had not yet come."

16:25 "Though I have been speaking figuratively, a time is coming when I will no longer use this kind of language but will tell you plainly about my Father."

16:32 "But a time is coming, and has come, when you will be scattered, each to his own home."

17:1 "Father, the time has come. Glorify your Son, that your Son may glorify you."

When warning his disciples that they will be scattered, Jesus discloses the secret of his equanimity in all circumstances. "You will leave me all alone. Yet I am not alone, for my Father is with me." In Cana, early in his ministry, and in Jerusalem at the end, in everything he yields himself to his Father's purpose and protection. Much, much later, Billy Graham draws on this same assurance in challenging people to accept Christ in his crusades: "You're not here by accident. You're here by the will of God."

Since Jesus was convinced God had sent him not to "call the righteous, but sinners," he went where they were. His conviviality offended sterner religious leaders (Paul Scherer says such people were "starched before they are washed"[3]) who couldn't help contrasting John's fasting disciples with Jesus' regular eaters. His defense was an analogy:

How can the guests of the bridegroom fast while he is with them? They cannot, so long as they have him with them. But the time will come when the bridegroom will be taken from them, and on that day they will fast (Mark 2:19).

In a sense, then, the radical scholars who think John 2 refers to Jesus' own wedding are correct, because in the kingdom of God he is the groom at every wedding, the espoused of every bride. At the Cana wedding feast Jesus is acting out the theme with which he opens his ministry ("The kingdom of God is at hand") and to which he will be faithful to the end.

There is another remarkable element in this event:

His Mother Takes His Compliance For Granted

"Do whatever he tells you," Mary instructs the servants. Does she presume because, as some scholars guess, he's related to the groom and therefore expected to help host? Or, as I suggested above, is it because he brought his disciples along, which means he was responsible for their contributions to the food and drink? Or is she to whom the angel appeared before his birth sensing that he can do something pretty special now, if he will? What better occasion could there be?

His address to her seems a little unusual. *"Gunai,"* that is, "Woman." We suspect he's teasing, being a little playful. We can't see the twinkle in his eye, but she can, as her order to the servants indicates. She knows he'll do something.

Interesting, isn't it, that Jesus, the one to whom "all authority in heaven and on earth" has been given, doesn't always have to be in charge? His willingness to please his mother on this occasion is not at odds with his authority. He is ever the *servant* of the Lord.

This conversation tickles me because it takes me back to my home. You noticed, didn't you, that Mary merely mentioned, "They have no more wine." A simple statement. Not even a request—certainly not an order. She used the same technique my mother employed when she wanted me to do something: "The dishes need to be washed." That's a simple declarative statement; there's no question, no request, no order. But let me tell you that I understood precisely what she meant: "Stop whatever else you are doing and get to the sink!" That's how mothers talk with sons. Thus Mary with Jesus. And he, too, understood. Hers was the power wielded by a woman who loves and knows her son. He'll want to help. That's what he's like. She can take him for granted.

Mostly we hate being taken for granted. Sometimes in marriage and in relationships we have at work or wherever, we resent people's assuming that we'll do this or that. They don't ask. They don't even order. They just presume. We wish they would think enough of us to ask. We fail to discern that they aren't treating us as nobodies. To the contrary, they know us well enough to have found us dependable. They trust us, as Mary trusts Jesus to keep the celebration going.

He Performs His First Sign at a Wedding Party

The word *sign* has special meaning to John. Signs aren't merely miracles or supernatural phenomena. They point beyond themselves or their executors to God's presence or purpose. This is Jesus' first, according to John, but not his last. It helps establish Jesus' credibility in the eyes of his disciples. Once Jesus has proved himself, though, he refuses to dabble in the miraculous just to titillate his audience. (See John 6:30-36.) Thus when Jesus turns water into wine, he is saying something about God (he is in this event) and about himself (I am empowered by God to do his purpose) and about the wedding party (it is important enough to warrant God's presence).

For how long have we ministers been alluding to the wedding at Cana as a part of our wedding rites? "As Jesus blessed the wedding at Cana . . ." we say, somehow tying this Palestinian festivity into God's blessing of the marriage of Adam and Eve in the beginning. If Jesus took the little refreshment crisis so seriously that he inaugurated his miracle-performing ministry there, then surely we must not take it lightly, either.

Every now and then the public becomes acutely aware of the importance of marriage and the difficulties two people incur when they become husband and wife. In recent years, presidential campaigns have unfailingly focused Americans' attention on it. In 1992 Bill Clinton's campaign against President Bush was seriously threatened in its early days by allegations of his marital unfaithfulness and his wife's apparent scorn of the traditional wifely role. Just exactly what was Clinton's commitment to marriage itself? And who exactly did Hillary think she was, demeaning the ladies at home baking cookies? In the midst of the flap, Margaret Carlson wrote some of the wisest words I read on the subject:

With her marriage being held up to the light for cracks, Hillary Clinton wonders how much of her intimate life a political spouse has to offer up. "My marriage is solid, full of love and friendship," she says, "but it's too profound to talk about glibly." In recent years, political reporters have come to think themselves as qualified to analyze a marriage as they are to sort out the deficit. But of course a marriage is infinitely more complicated.[4]

More complicated and more critical to the prosperity of a nation.

The French author Honore de Balzac paid superficial tribute to marriage's high estate in his *Physiologie Du Mariage* when he commented, "It is easier to be a lover than a husband for the simple reason that it is more difficult to be witty every day than to say pretty things from time to time." More than pretty sayings are at stake of course. Balzac touches the surface, but only the surface, of the demands to be met when two persons contract to love, honor, cherish, help, forgive, entertain, and serve one other for a lifetime. In some ways what they are undertaking seems more miraculous than what Jesus did with the water he turned to wine.

The hope, of course, is that one day the bride can look back and say with Anne Bradstreet,

If ever two were one, then surely we.
If ever man were lov'd by wife, then thee;
If ever wife was happy in a man,
Compare with me ye women if you can.

In some respects, I suppose, you could say that Jesus' miracle here is not a very significant one, especially when compared with healing a blind person or summoning Lazarus back from the grave. But it surely seemed so to the wedding hosts. Jesus was taking them, the wedding, and the guests seriously. And because of what he did, they took him more seriously. Something wonderful had happened that day.

Wonderful. This word appears often on these pages. A Christian often is stopped by the sheer wonder of life in Christ. He's like King Broda of Scotland, who was listening to St. Brandon preach one day and was sufficiently moved to ask, "If I accept your gospel and become Christ's man, what can I expect to find?"

St. Brandon's reply is one I could give because of what has happened to me and to many whose walk with the Lord I have observed. "If you accept my gospel and become Christ's man, you will stumble upon wonder upon wonder, and every wonder true."[5]

The greatest wonder of all, of course, is the Christian's suddenly clear insight into the significance of little things. Jesus' turning of water to wine is perhaps not his most earth-shaking sign. It hasn't been in life's great traumas that faith has been strengthened in us, either. It has been in the small things, the seemingly insignificant moments, that our most profound spiritual insights have come to us. We see the touch of God where others find nothing of note.

Michael Lindvall tells of one such day, when two very ordinary situations shone more brightly than anything else that happened. One of them was in Harry's barber shop. Lindvall doesn't know exactly what he said, but whatever it was touched a nerve, and Harry started to talk. And talk. About being a kid and what a pain it was, and about his father. "My old man," he called him, though Harry was a seventy-year-old himself. The haircut was finished, but Harry wasn't. His scissors in one hand and a comb in the other, resting both hands on Lindvall's shoulders, Harry talked about his unhappy childhood, his abusive father, the frightening Saturday nights when his "old man" came home drunk, about the love and hate he felt for his father. He had never told anybody about this before, not in sixty years. His mother never did.

While he talked, Michael reached to his shoulders and held Harry's hands, looking at him in the barber's mirrors in a way they couldn't have looked at one another face to face. Harry's eyes reddened. Michael told him that when you forgive somebody, it doesn't mean you are approving what he did.

The second important event happened that evening after a church meeting that ended fairly early. The kids were waiting up for their bedtime story and kisses. He felt more like plopping in front of the television but went upstairs and found his two little girls fighting sleep, their book ready, a slip of yellow construction paper marking the spot where they had stopped reading the night before. So the tired minister read to them from chapter six of *Ramona the Pest*. They were sound asleep before he finished. He kissed them and sat at the edge of the bed and said their prayers for them.

Then it came to him. All the meetings of the last few days, all the sermons, the programs, the multitudinous duties of a busy pastor, all his "busy-ness" faded beside the really important things he did: he touched Harry's hands, and he read chapter six of *Ramona the Pest* to two of the most important people in the world.[6]

Little things. To see the little things as God sees them is to experience life as celebration, as joy, as thanksgiving, as gladness in being alive. In the grand scheme of things, keeping a wedding party going doesn't seem such a big deal. Neither does listening to an old man's reminiscences of his unhappy childhood, nor reading a goodnight story to a couple of little girls. Little things they are. But what was it Jesus taught us? If you're faithful in little things, he will make it possible for you to become faithful in much. He practiced what he preached.

That's why he attended a wedding party and replenished the refreshments for some friends, to keep the festivities going. A pretty trivial demonstration of the Messiah's power.

But to the bride and groom and their families, what could have seemed more important?

[1]Northrop Frye, *Words with Power*. New York: Harcourt Brace Jovanovich, 1990, p. 105.

[2]Ari L. Goldman, *The Search for God at Harvard*. New York: Time Books, Random House, 1991, pp. 188-191.

[3]In "The Minister's Workshop," *Christianity Today*, September 13, 1963.

[4]"Hillary Clinton: Partner as Much as Wife," *Time*, January 27, 1992, p. 19.

[5]Marshall Leggett, *Genuine Ministers*. Joplin, Missouri: College Press, 1989, p. 101.

[6]Michael L. Lindvall, *The Good News from North Haven*. New York: Doubleday, 1991, pp. 24, 25.

Chapter 3

Destination Unknown

Luke 5:27-32

How many times the thought has caused me simply to stop and shake my head. It often has happened when Joy and I have found ourselves in another part of the world, but sometimes it happens in the privacy of our home, when I'm sitting at the computer answering a letter or preparing a sermon. How did I get here? How is it possible that this life I am leading now is so far different from, so much more exciting than, anything I ever imagined when I was growing up in Tillamook, or attending college in Eugene, or even in those first few years of ministry in Portland?

Little did I know when I accepted Jesus' call that I was being invited to a destination unknown. Unknown to me, but certainly within his purview. All I have had to do is trust him. He has taken care of all the arrangements.

Perhaps I should begin at the beginning, not with my own call but with the concept of calling. What is it, anyway? Roman Catholics have helped all Christians to understand the word. *Vocation* is the one they use, derived from the Latin word for "calling." In the stilted language of *Webster's Third International Dictionary*, the first definition of *vocation* is

> a summons from God to an individual or group to undertake the obligations and perform the duties of a particular task or function in life: a divine call to a place of service to others in accordance with the divine plan.

Thus we speak of Christ's call to salvation, his call to service, his call to the ministry, and in the case of Luke 5, his call to a particular person to leave his sordid trade and to become a disciple.

Always Christ's call is a bid to follow him, which means a leaving as well as a following, not an easy thing to do when, like Levi's, yours has been a lucrative career. It's a challenge to renounce softness, to take up service, even sacrifice. It's always a dare to walk away from security into insecurity, and beyond security to the security on the other side of insecurity, where joy awaits the one who dares.

When Jesus said, "Follow me," Levi got up and left, left everything. We have some difficulty following Jesus because we have such difficulty leaving. We're tied to our possessions, our traditions, and our comforts. We don't like leave-taking unless we're certain we can get right back to the same place, like a dear friend who loves to travel. She will go anywhere in the world so long as she can be home by bedtime. We are eager to follow Jesus, so long as there's no real leaving.

Christ's "Follow me" is more than a leaving; it is also a "calling forth" of what is already in you, perhaps only as an embryo, undeveloped—enough for a start yet nowhere near enough for the finish. Levi (or Matthew, as he is better known) was a tax collector, and some of his fellow disciples mere fishermen. Not much to build on there. To the ordinary eye they were most unremarkable men, not the stuff of apostleship. But then, he who called them didn't look with ordinary eyes. He saw what was within, ready to be used for the Lord. He does not call us to be what we can't become; he expects rather that we offer what we have.

I heard the call to follow Jesus as a disciple when I was nine. By the time I was twelve, I was certain he wanted me to be a preacher. My father may have played a role in preparing me. In addition to seeing that his family was in church every Sunday, he also encouraged each of us to develop our talents. We all worked in his grocery store, where we learned the rudiments of the business. My sister, always social and popular, became even more so as she bantered with the customers. My brother's mechanical aptitude emerged early, and our parents encouraged him. What should become of me they little doubted. Dad, especially, thought I should do something with my mouth, since he was himself pretty tongue-tied before a crowd. He couldn't imagine how I could speak before an audience. He teased me, but proudly, as he explained to the customers, "The boy's not good for anything but talking," adding, "Yes, he kissed the blarney stone."

Some of the greatest spiritual advisers in my life, on the other hand, cannot preach. They do many things well, but speaking isn't among them. Their ministry has taken other expressions, and the kingdom of God is richer because they are in it. In a genuine sense, they have a *vocation,* and they serve with distinction. They are like Levi, whom Jesus did not call to preach, but to follow him. What that meant Levi would only discover in the following.

To move a person like Levi requires a call, a summons from beyond the merely human. What other man could have lured him from his accounting table? The bid had to come from the one who would not be dissuaded by Levi's reputation or connections, from someone who knew how much more Levi could be than he had ever been, someone who saw beneath the reality of his immediate situation to the possibilities God had planted in him, potentialities beyond Levi's self-knowing, which could come to light only as he offered himself to the one who called.

Left alone, we don't ever call ourselves. We are too certain of what—and how little—there is within to be called out. We use only what's readily available to us; we live on the surface. The call assumes there's more to us than we think, and that it is needed by the Caller, who has the power to summon it from our depths.

The danger of a calling is not in hearing the summons, but in not answering it. It isn't merely a refusing of the one who calls or the denial of the request itself but a rejection of the possibilities, a giving in to the dread of danger, a foreshortening of destiny.

Refusal to answer the call is a personal negation that unspiritual persons never even suspect they have suffered. Levi could have kept at his tax business; the fishermen could have kept fishing. They would have had sufficient income. Their social acceptance would not have suffered. They would have been safe in their routine, mere faces in the crowd, unnamed in history books. Jesus didn't require them to become fishers of men. He just invited. They came. Can you help wondering whether he invited others who refused, their momentary opportunity for everlasting glory spurned? The disaster is not in what they suffered but in what they missed.

So I ponder, as I sit at my computer, what would have happened to me if I had said no? Surely mine is the query of every person who has heard God's soft-spoken invitation. No threats if we refuse, no gruesome pictures of the dire consequences if we choose not to accept. Just the call. It has made all the difference.

So much difference, in fact, that I could hardly believe my eyes when reading the letters to the editor in a *Christianity Today* some time ago. (I must have been agitated. I failed to note the date of the issue. It's on page six, though.) Somebody named L. Bert Ramsey of Medicine Hat, Alberta, would not appreciate my idyllic view of ministry. "I would sooner encourage gifted persons to drink bleach," he fumes, "than bid them to enter such a joyless profession as pastoral ministry. Simple compassion forbids it."

His anger is harmless. He isn't the one to "bid them to enter" anyway. That's the Lord's task. And it isn't to a *profession* that he bids one enter. Perhaps this misunderstanding explains Mr. Ramsey's rancor. As professions go, the ministry isn't among the top ten. But Jesus doesn't call us to professional status. He couldn't; he never had it himself. He never achieved more than amateur rank, and to participate as amateurs (who work or play for the love of it and not for money or power or recognition) he calls us.

Since everybody else works for money, recognition, or power, though, it's no small thing to answer this unusual call. You have to be able to trust that life can be satisfactory on some other than the usual terms.

Learning to Trust

Trusting doesn't come easily, either. Oh, it does in the beginning. The newborn infant recognizes and trusts its mother. Earlier, in the womb, there was security, protection, sustenance, all provided by the mother. Trust was natural.

Then came birth, the harsh passage from the sustaining womb to the strange and often hostile new world, from dependence to a form of independence. The glare, the noise, the new demands, commands, the strange hands groping, forcing, the swift motions, the ups and downs and sudden starts and stops. What a shock to the nine-month-old system.

Whom can he turn to, whom can he trust? Only the mother, and even she is not always there.

This is what maturation is all about, isn't it? It is a weaning from dependence and trust to independence and guarded distrust.

This is also what maturation is all about: a returning to dependence and trust, now enlightened, selectively cautious.

It comes from opening one's eyes to what's around and seeing through to what's behind it. As C. H. Spurgeon so poetically expressed it,

We, by faith, perceive the hand of the Lord giving to every blade of grass its own drop of dew, and to every young raven its meat. We see the present power of God in the flight of every sparrow, and hear His goodness in the song of every lark. We believe that "the earth is the Lord's, and the fulness thereof"; and we go forth into it, not as into the domains of Satan where light comes not, nor into a chaos where rule is unknown, nor into a boiling sea where fate's resistless billows shipwreck mortals at their will; but we walk boldly on, having God within us and around us, living and moving and having our being in Him, and so, by faith, we dwell in a temple of providence and grace wherein everything doth speak of His glory.[1]

Trust may begin without any consciousness of God but with a feeling, as Tagore puts it, that "everything lifts up strong hands after perfection."[2] We want more than the humdrum, the merely sensate. We begin to trust that there is something, Someone, behind what our senses can know. We marvel over the miracle of birth and believe it more than accidental that a particular sperm united with a special egg to produce this unique person, me. We contemplate the other end of earthly existence and resist the conclusion that all we are is what's trapped in this body and anchored to this planet. Surely there is more, there is another mode of existence prepared for us by—Someone.

Jean Paul Sartre devoted his life to propagating his special brand of atheistic existentialism, but apparently his philosophy didn't hold. As an old man he is reported to have said, "I do not feel that I am the product of chance, a speck of dust in universe, but someone who was expected, prepared, prefigured. In short, a being whom only a Creator could put here; and this of a creating hand refers to God." Stephen Board wryly comments on Sartre's eleventh-hour talk of God: "Whatever can't be believed all your life will fail as a full-journey ticket."[3]

Henrik Ibsen's Master Builder, the forceful Dr. Stockman, would insist that neither God nor companions are necessary in this world, "This is what I have discovered, you see: the strongest man in the world is he who stands most alone,"[4] but Dr. Stockman met defeat at the hands of his own ego. Not much comfort in his philosophy.

You can neither go it alone, nor can you place all your faith in others who are just like you. God remains the only viable alternative. If God is in the beginning and God is at the end ("the Alpha and the Omega" of Revelation 1:8), then God is undoubtedly present for the present. This doesn't sound like a resounding confession of faith, but it's the starting place of trust. It's the tentative trust of one who has trusted in possessions, power, human relationships, self-sufficiency—and found them all lacking. Either one must live without trust or find one who is trustworthy.

Learning to Trust Jesus

This talk of trust in God has really been about trusting in Jesus, since his call to Levi has elicited this meditation. I have generalized, thinking of the progress in three phases: 1) learning to trust again, to recapture the ability to place one's faith in something or someone, as a baby has faith in the mother; 2) coming to think of that something or someone as God, the giver and sustainer of life; 3) accepting that God has revealed himself to humankind in the person of Jesus of Nazareth.

It was to Jesus that Levi entrusted himself. Undoubtedly already a believer in God, Levi saw something in Jesus that invoked his trust, and he "left everything and followed him."

I can't ever read this passage without thinking of Shakespeare's King Lear, in that scene in which the Duke pledges his loyalty to his puzzled king, who wants to know why he would follow him when all other courtiers except the fool have deserted him. "Because there is that in thy face which I would fain call lord," he said. You look like a king! So did Jesus to Levi.

What adventures lay in store for the tax collector? What should we infer from Luke's report that Levi "left everything"? Is this a hint concerning the cost of discipleship, the risk that trust in Jesus entails? "It isn't safe to believe in the God of the Bible," Paul Scherer cautions, but then issues a larger warning: "Indeed it isn't safe to live!" Some people foolishly look to God to secure them against all risk. To do so would be to inoculate them against life itself. Scherer's case is to the point:

> Security at its peak is little more than sterility. Only insecurity has some chance of being creative. It can never be overcome. It can only be resolved into some other brave risk for us to take. If your life is dull, you haven't been taking any. If it's uninteresting, you've made it so. And you are not likely to help things much by acquiring a few added "interests" in the shape of luncheons and lectures and book clubs. Life doesn't want to be safe. It doesn't want to absorb something. It wants to create something. It wants to breast some slope. It wants to be gallant. Insecurity is its heritage.[5]

Former British Prime Minister Benjamin Disraeli learned this lesson well. "One must run risks in life, or else it would be as dull as death."[6] Not only did he test himself against the hazards of national political leadership, but in later life he forced his body to combat a host of illnesses, including bronchial asthma and gout, overcoming severe pain and fighting for breath to perform his Cabinet duties. Friends and physicians counseled him to take it easy, to husband his limited strength rather than spend himself so carelessly, but he feared dullness more than death.

To trust Jesus is to court adventure. It is to offer yourself for service, not knowing in advance where your volunteering will take you. That "not knowing" is what causes us to hold back. It's far easier to believe in some nebulous god, one distant enough to make no demands on us, than to leave everything and follow Jesus.

I like William Sloane Coffin's picture of our reaction to Jesus' call. He compares it to a frequent scene in an old vaudeville show, that part in which the inevitable magician tells his inevitable jokes, like the one about the dentist and the manicurist who got married and spent the rest of their lives fighting tooth and nail, with the inevitable appeal for respect, "You should show more respect for my jokes, they're older than you are. My act is terrific: it not only answers the question who killed vaudeville, but re-enacts the crime before your eyes." The jokes stop when he asks the man in the end seat to come forward. You look around to see who the patsy is this time, but you hear him say, "No, not you, you—the gentleman turning around," and to your horror you realize he means you. You're furious. You didn't pay your money for this. You paid to be a spectator, and now this fellow is calling you to take part in the act.[7]

Something like this happened to me in 1990. Joy and I flew to Hawaii to celebrate our thirtieth anniversary. Arriving on Kuai late in the afternoon, we freshened up in our rooms and headed directly to the restaurant. We went for food but were pleased to learn there would be a Hawaiian floor show. We enjoyed it up to the minute when, after a hula exhibition, the master of ceremonies announced it was time for group participation. I quickly turned in my chair, hoping to avert his eyes. It did no good. "You back there, you with your back to me." I was summoned. On stage I proved to be amazingly uncoordinated. I couldn't learn the hula. My wife's obvious enjoyment at my plight did not assuage my humiliation. I, who intended to be a spectator, had been forced to be a participant.

You can believe in God and never hear yourself called up to the stage. You can be a bystander forever. When Jesus says, "Follow me," he is inviting, not coercing. You can stay in your tax booth or last-row seat or at your restaurant table forever. But you have to decide to do so. The choice is put before you: Will you trust him or won't you?

Who does he think he is, that he can make such a demand on you?

Who does he think you are, that he can expect so much?

Celebrating Trust After Distrust

Life's great rewards don't go to the spectators. They are awarded to the risk-takers, the performers, the trusting believers.

Following Jesus is like taking the plunge into a cold river. You can't just dip your big toe in, or try to walk deeper into it an inch at a time. A tentative disciple is an oxymoron, a contradiction in terms. Look at the average church member: respectable, financially secure, conservative in taste and convictions, an unexceptional, uninteresting statistic. While you are at it, look a little more carefully. You'll find true disciples in almost every congregation. You'll recognize them by their quiet zeal for living, their quick smiles, their busy but uncluttered schedules, their rich friendships, their readiness to dare, to try, to give. They speak more of the future than the past; they anticipate an exciting trip or project and they speak enthusiastically of their interest in religion and poetry and music and sports and politics and art. In fact, they seem to be interested in everything and everybody, just like the One whom they are so eagerly following. Without exception, if you ask them to explain this generalized fervor, they'll refer you to the Lord who called them and whose call they have answered. That has made all the difference.

They have taken seriously Jesus' promise: "If you cling to your life, you will lose it; but if you give it up for me, you will save it" (Matthew 10:39, *The Living Bible*). Tom Sine rightly attributes the exhilaration we experience in serving Jesus (what he calls "the celebration of servanthood") to our having discovered the "right-side-up values of the kingdom" that are to be found in giving ourselves away, and he speaks of the "heightened joy" we discover "from incarnating the countercultural values of the kingdom."[8] The example he uses to illustrate this reversal of values is of a young couple Jan and Jeff who had only been Christians a year when they made a very costly decision. During Jan's oral surgery three years earlier the surgeon had broken her jaw. Since he refused to accept any responsibility for his obvious blunder, she and Jeff filed suit to reclaim damages and lawyer fees. The case dragged on for three years.

Then, just two weeks before the insurance company was to have sent their settlement check, the couple decided that as Christ's disciples they could not take money from a lawsuit against the oral surgeon. Love and forgiveness were their only recourse. They dropped the charges, forfeiting their fifteen- to twenty-thousand-dollar settlement. They still had to pay their attorney four thousand dollars.

The result? Sine says he has never seen two happier people. "They were jubilant because they had obeyed the teachings of Jesus and were learning to trust God for every aspect of their lives—including raising four thousand dollars to pay off their attorney."

Had Joy and I not made similar decisions, I might have doubted Sine's claims. But we can add our own testimony: there is nothing more rejuvenating than to do the right thing for the right reasons. Whenever we have followed Jesus at some personal risk or cost, the reward has outweighed both the risk and the cost.

Because of our experience, I wasn't surprised at someone else's testimony. A friend shared Philip Hallie's *Lest Innocent Blood Be Shed* with me. It's a dramatic account of the efforts of one little French village to save Jewish refugees from the Nazis in World War II. Led by their intrepid pastor, people who had never had a taste of heroism in their lives regularly risked everything in the rescue effort. The pastor's wife later explained LeChambon's extraordinary effort in simple but revealing terms. "You know," she said, "saving refugees was a *hobby* for the people of LeChambon! Oh, yes! It was a hobby in LeChambon."9

An amazing word—but precise. Their love-labors (they were amateurs, remember) became a kind of play, a refreshing pastime that rescued them from the stupefying routines of everyday existence. They had lost themselves in the kind of labor to which Christ's love calls us.

Celebrating in Spite of...

I hope by now I have made it clear that as disciples who have answered Christ's call we will have a joyful life, but it's joy in spite of. . . . In spite of danger, risk, cost, exhaustion, and the petty demands of petty people. The joy comes in reorienting life to Christ and away from self, to giving and away from getting, from controlling to being controlled by Another. But away from irritations and problems? Never. We keep on following, *in spite of.*

Especially in spite of what people think. In a recent capital funds campaign in our church, our consultant, James Varner, challenged us with a little wisdom he had picked up in his work. "People of faith," he read,

CARE more than other people think is WISE,
RISK more than other people think is SAFE,
DREAM more than other people think is PRACTICAL,
EXPECT more than other people think is POSSIBLE.

He's right on all four counts. Only one other line needs to be added. People of faith also

CELEBRATE more than other people think is SANE.

So we conclude this not very theological exploration of the meaning of a call to discipleship. It is, in the end, a call to fun, to celebration, to occasional hilarity. It is, perhaps most of all, a call to energy, to perpetually renewing activity, to the "high" of the perspiring marathon runner, gasping for breath but exuding vitality.

If you've been called to fish for men, angling for fish just can't suffice. I grew up among fishermen who had answered the call of the sea. For them there could never be too many fish. As long as their legs could stand in the swells, they fished. It was never a pastime nor even a job. It was a vocation. One doesn't retire from a vocation. It keeps calling. Real fishermen keep answering. You see lots of old salts down at the harbor, studying the tides and the winds, ready to return to the sea as soon as the conditions are right.

If you've been called to fish for men, there are never too many men, either. Each is unique. Some are more interesting than others, but not a one is without some fascination, some challenge, some point of human contact for you, something that will enlarge you. So you, too, cannot retire from your fishing. You'll be on the lookout for men and women whom you can "catch" for the Lord for as long as you live.

The call to discipleship comes from the deeps, not from the distance. Frederick Buechner says, "The place God calls you to is the place where your deep gladness and the world's deep hunger meet."[10] Though Andrew and Peter and James and John left their boats to follow Jesus, they did not move to Rome. Levi left his money table, but he did not leave his home territory. Beware the lure of the exotic, the romance of the pilgrimage. A call is not a quest. You are not searching; you have been found. The treasure is not elsewhere. You are the treasure. The bumper sticker campaign announced a few years ago, "I found it." That's not quite the Gospel. "I've been found" is what happened. Now I can help find others.

We used to sing, "Brighten the corner where you are," and, "This little light of mine, I'm gonna let it shine. . . . All around the neighborhood, I'm gonna let it shine." Good songs, worth remembering when the urge to wander hits. If I don't shine here, what delusion makes me think a move will make me brighter? Jesus' call to discipleship has next to nothing to do with geography.

Next to nothing, but not nothing. Because if I am unwilling to leave, I can't very well follow. The correct response must be like Isaiah's: "Here am I. Send me." Removal to another location may be ahead for me. It's just that the decision isn't mine. It's the Caller's call.

What do you think would have happened to James and John, Peter and Andrew, Levi and the rest if, when Jesus bade them come, they had politely refused the invitation?

Nothing. They'd have stayed with their boats or tax booth, plying their trade, eating and drinking and working and contributing their bit. And, as the world measures such things, it would have been all right.

But no cause for celebrating.

[1]C. H. Spurgeon, *An All-Round Ministry*. Pasadena, Texas: Pilgrim Publications, 1973, pp. 5, 6.

[2]Quoted in E. Stanley Jones, *A Song of Ascents*. Nashville: Abingdon, 1968, p. 373.

[3]Stephen Board, "Editor's Ink," *Eternity*, July-August 1983, p. 3.

[4]Henrik Ibsen, *The Enemy of the People*.

[5]Paul Scherer, *The Word God Sent*. New York: Harper and Row, p. 209.

[6]Chad Walsh, *Behold the Glory*. New York: Harper and Brothers, 1955, pp. 27, 28.

[7]William Sloane Coffin, Jr., "The Call," Franklin H. Littell, ed., *Sermons to Intellectuals*, New York: Macmillan, 1963, pp. 12, 13.

[8]Tom Sine, *The Mustard Seed Conspiracy*. Waco: Word, 1981, p. 119.

[9]Philip Hallie, *Lest Innocent Blood Be Shed*. New York: Harper and Row, 1979, p. 195.

[10]Frederick Buechner, *Wishful Thinking—A Theological ABC*. Quoted in *Leadership*, Summer 1990, p. 19.

Chapter 4

How Do You Feed Five Thousand People?

Mark 6:30-44

No miracle of Jesus captures our imagination more vividly than his feeding of the five thousand. We are not alone in our amazement. This compelling incident is re-lated in every one of the four Gospels, as if each writer sensed he was recounting something of supreme impor-tance.

Subsequent commentators have so analyzed and theo-rized and speculated about the event that there really is nothing new to be added to the literature about it. They have labored to be certain we are aware of . . .

the people's eagerness to hear Jesus' every word. The crowds pressed themselves on him; he couldn't escape even to get a little much-deserved rest.

Jesus' compassion on them. They were "like sheep without a shepherd." He cared about their spiritual lives, hence his careful teaching; he also cared about their physical well-being, hence his willingness to feed them.

His disciples' concern about him—and their presump-tion. "Send the people away," they urged him. You need rest. There are too many of them for us to take care of. They've demanded too much; you've given enough. Send them away. Not unlike a modern President's "handlers," they believe they know what's best for him—and don't hesitate to say so.

Jesus' challenge: "**You** give them something to eat." They weren't prepared for this unexpected turn of events.

The people's inadequacy. They couldn't meet their own needs. Five loaves and two fish were no better than nothing in the face of the overwhelming need. Besides, they weren't an organized group, just a teeming crowd. Who would take charge?

Jesus' organizational skill. The Bible writers make nothing special of his arranging of the thousands of people into manageable groups and his skill in delegating the distribution task to his disciples, but later students of leadership have made much of it.

All these things are worthy of the attention scholars have given them, but our subject is celebration, so we will bypass the more popular themes. We want to focus on what caused this incident to receive such attention from the Gospel writers, and why anybody who knows about Jesus knows about this miracle. For us it's the perfect symbol of the abundant life Jesus promises his disciples ("I am come that they might have life and that they might have it more abundantly"—John 10:10, KJV).

It's the end of the episode that gives us the clue to its importance. The writers pay close attention to the part of a successful social gathering we'd rather skip: the cleanup. At the beginning there are five loaves and two fishes; at the end, twelve baskets full of leftovers. That's abundance.

Celebrating the Lord's Abundance

The movement in the narrative is *from insufficiency to surplus.* If you were coming on the story for the first time, you'd never predict the twelve basketfuls.

It is the common testimony of Christians after a lifetime with the Lord that in the beginning there was struggle, scarcity, and no little anxiety about tomorrow. In the end, however, there is amazement that they who began with so little ended with so much more than they ever dreamed of. They have more than enough. In addition to having all their needs met, they now have the joy of sharing their abundance. Paul's promise has been fulfilled in their lives: "You will be made rich in every way so that you can be generous on every occasion..." (2 Corinthians 9:11).

Virginia Stem Owens says she's convinced "no one should be allowed to claim faith who knows where his next meal is coming from or where he will sleep tonight."[1] Faith begins in insufficiency, in not knowing and not having; it matures in trust through obedience and hope. It gives the Lord a chance to reward it.

Canon Peter Green, for nearly forty years a parish priest in Salford, England, was honored near the end of his long service when he was given the Freedom of the City of Salford. The Dean of Manchester described him as "the greatest parish priest in England—more than that, the most human parish priest in England." Green himself traced his Christianity back to his youth, when he had asked a friend what religion meant to him. "It's waking up in the middle of the night," he answered, "remembering that you belong to God, and turning over and going to sleep happy because of it."[2]

That's faith.

The movement is *from helplessness to strength*. "That would take eight months of a man's wages," they said. They didn't have that much to spare. They probably didn't have that much, period. Who were they among so many? And when they received the pitiful offering of five loaves and two fish, what could it do against so many hungry mouths?

They asked the questions, but Jesus gave the orders. "You give them something.... Go and see how many loaves you have.... Have the people sit down in groups...." Without wavering, he quietly took charge.

The very extremity of the situation gave Jesus his chance. If the crowd had had sufficient resources, Jesus would not have taken control. As long as we are satisfied with our own strength, he lets us enjoy ourselves. It is only, as Paul discovered, when we are weak that we are strong.[3]

Augustine, in an oft-quoted statement, asserts that "God wants to give us something, but cannot, because our hands are full—there's nowhere for him to put it." But when we come to him with empty hands, or with a few loaves and fish, then he can and does give out of his own strength.

The movement of the narrative is, in other words, *from human concern to divine response.* Lest we be critical of the disciples, let us at least admit that they've taken the first step, which is to be concerned. They are not calloused or insensitive regarding either Jesus or the crowd. Their ministry with Jesus has undoubtedly influenced them positively. Another testimony of longtime Christians, especially as they recall the early days and the change that has come over them, is that the Lord has stretched their circle of concern. Many whose plights they hadn't even noticed before are now in their prayers and on their list of projects.

They usually speak also of an overpowering sense of helplessness, often accompanied by despondency over their inability to relieve others' suffering. Their growing concern for others has led to a growing consciousness of their own inadequacy. They feel too weak, too poor. They are lighting the proverbial candle in the darkness, but the flame glimmers feebly.

On many occasions I have heard Knofel Staton, my longtime friend and predecessor as president of Pacific Christian College, exhort crowds to trust in the Lord's ability. God has power in abundance, he assures them. Then he turns to Ephesians 3:20 and reads,

"Now unto him that is able to do...above all that we ask or think according to the power that worketh in us...." Then Dr. Staton pauses and starts again.

"Now unto him that is able to do...*abundantly* above...." Then he starts again.

"Now unto him that is able to do...*exceeding abundantly* above...." Still he hasn't finished emphasizing this incredible proclamation of God's ability.

"Now unto him that is *able to do exceeding abundantly above all* that we ask or think, *according to the power that worketh in us,* unto him be glory in the church by Christ Jesus throughout all ages, world without end. Amen." By the time he has finished reading these two verses, no one in the audience can doubt the source of the Christian's power. We are often feeble, inadequate, poor and weak, but *he is able.*

On each of the times I have heard Knofel read this Scripture in his dramatic way, he has blessed me with the reminder I regularly need in my work. The challenges are too large, the needs too great, and my personal resources too puny for me to hope to succeed on my own. He has more than enough to accomplish what he has called me—and you—to do.

Robert Coles recounts the experience of a young girl who was among the few brave black children who faced angry mobs of whites in the early days of school desegregation in the South. "I was alone," one North Carolina girl of eight told him in 1962,

> and those [segregationist] people were screaming, and suddenly I saw God smiling, and I smiled. A woman was standing there [near the school door], and she shouted at me, "Hey, you little nigger, what you smiling at?" I looked right at her face, and I said, "At God." Then she looked up at the sky, and then she looked at me, and she didn't call me any more names.[4]

"Yea, though I walk through the valley of the shadow of death, I will fear no evil; for thou art with me; thy rod and thy staff they comfort me" (Psalm 23:4, KJV).

Celebrating the Believer's Abundance in the Lord

Pardon me if I read a little into the text. I can't help imagining the fun the disciples must have had passing out the food to the hungry crowd. Of course, what they were sharing wasn't their own. But then, the Bible teaches us that no matter what we share, it isn't our own. God is the owner.

The greatest joy in life does not come from receiving but from giving. I suspect the disciples were receiving a stupendous blessing from assuaging the hunger of those who had walked so far to see and hear Jesus.

A long time ago I ceased being impressed by people's possessions. There is an old definition of wealth that I endorse: A person shows his wealth not in what he has but in what he gives. On that day, the disciples were experiencing the flush of wealth.

In his ministry Jesus took pains to equip his disciples to share their abundance. In other words, he first provided the abundance. In the instance of feeding the 5,000, they had little or nothing to give, so he provided the food for them. A quick review of his training program makes it evident that Jesus was determined that they should lack nothing that would help them help others.

• When he dispatched his disciples by twos, he *"gave them authority* to drive out evil spirits and to heal every disease and sickness. . . . They drove out many demons and anointed many sick people with oil and healed them" (Mark 6:7, 13). They had often observed him healing others; now it was their turn. In Luke 9, Jesus feeds the five thousand immediately after the disciples return from this trial mission. Then in chapter ten he sends out seventy-two of his followers for their "internship" in ministry.

• When he startled his friends by washing their feet during their last supper before his crucifixion, he let them know that even in such a servile act as that one, they are to imitate him. He has previously empowered them to teach, to heal, to cast out demons; now *he is empowering (and challenging) them* to act the part of a servant when necessary.

• The greatest example of Jesus' empowering his followers comes, of course, at the end of his own ministry and the beginning of theirs. Out of his abundant authority he has ministered ("All authority in heaven and on earth has been given to me"); now *he bestows that same sufficiency on them* ("Therefore go and make disciples of all nations. . ."). They are now on their own, since he is departing this earth. Yet they are not completely alone, either ("And surely I am with you always, to the very end of the age"; Matthew 28:18-20). Wherever they are, he will be with them. They will have all the power they will ever need ("You will receive power when the Holy Spirit comes on you. . ."; Acts 1:8).

The rest, as they say, is history. As the record of the apostles' early ministry testifies, these heretofore rather ordinary men accomplish extraordinary feats through the abundance of their power. The Lord had provided for them abundantly.

The earliest Christians were caught up in the apostles' enthusiasm, and Luke reports that

> day by day, attending the temple together and breaking bread in their homes, they partook of food with *glad and generous* hearts, praising God and having favor with all the people (Acts 2:46, 47, RSV).

I often quote this passage and point out the italicized words. Gladness and generosity are inseparable. Like the apostles, the new Christians were experiencing the abundance of God's blessings. Out of their abundance they too were giving and thus enjoying themselves immensely. This, in fact, is a good description of the Christian's walk: abundance overflowing in generosity.

Without both abundance and generosity the Christian walk is crippled.

A latter-day observer of the human personality applies the principle beyond the confines of the Christian community. Dr. Karl Meninger of Kansas' famed Meninger Clinic has written, "Money-giving is a very good criterion of a person's mental health. Generous people are rarely mentally ill people."[5] And as someone else has commented, "When we try to reach happiness on cheap terms, what we get is bound to be cheap. That is why pleasure seekers in any age are always the most bored and dissatisfied people on earth."[6]

The tightwad caricatured in the following verses has missed the whole fun of the abundant life.

> Once there was a Christian,
> He had a pious look,
> His consecration was complete,
> Except his pocketbook.
>
> He'd put a nickel in the plate,
> And then with might and main
> He'd sing, "When we asunder part
> It gives us inward pain."[7]

Almost every year for the thirty-five years of my ministry I have taken a full month to preach stewardship sermons, and with very few exceptions I have introduced the series with a disclaimer that goes something like this: "My primary goal in these sermons is not to get you to give more money to the church but to help you to attain more joy in your life. This series is about commitment to Jesus Christ, about the choice we all must make between Mammon and God, about the gladness that comes through—and only through—generosity. Remember, Jesus came to give us life eternal and abundant. These sermons have to do with your abundant life, and what to do with your abundance so that yours will be a life of celebration."

Most of the congregation listen with skepticism. They aren't ready to risk tithing, to trust God to use their remaining ninety percent better than they are managing their hundred percent. But each year there are a few who hear me and are ready to trust. They are the newly joyful ones.

For several years I've been pondering Albert Einstein's warning regarding money:

> I am absolutely convinced that no wealth in the world can help humanity forward, even in the hands of the most devoted worker in this cause. The example of great and pure individuals is the only thing that can lead us to noble thoughts and deeds. Money only appeals to selfishness and irresistibly invites abuse.
>
> Can anyone imagine Moses, Jesus, or Gandhi armed with the money-bags of Carnegie?[8]

No, no one can. On the other hand, although these great personages had little or no money themselves, they fully understood the necessity of making use of some form of currency. Even Jesus relied on the generosity of the women who gave money to his cause. (See Luke 8:3.) Einstein's warning is well placed, though. Money does appeal to selfishness and invites abuse. When money is used to further the Lord's cause, however, the generosity with which it is given engenders a spirit of gladness. We don't celebrate money, but we can certainly celebrate with it.

The Biblical minimum for giving of our means is, as I mentioned above, the tithe. Americans, who like to boast of big-heartedness and ready openhandedness, pretty consistently give about one-fifth that amount (as measured by the percentage of the gross national product) to all causes, a figure that has remained constant since 1830, through war and peace, depression and prosperity.

> Economic recessions and swings in the financial markets do not seem to stem the steady increase in giving. For example, a study of five major stock-market downturns between 1962 and 1987 showed that charitable giving overall continued to rise in the years of market decline, even though households were poorer. People continued to give about the same share of their wealth in spite of major losses in the stock market in each of these years.[9]

Given America's relative wealth when measured against the third world, and the average American's abundance when contrasted with the poverty of the nation's bottom third, one can hardly congratulate us on the overflowing of our abundance. Perhaps that is why, to reflect on Dr. Meninger's comment, mental illness is on the rise. We have the abundance; we lack the overflowing. When we withhold the generosity, gladness is withheld from us.

Celebrating the Crowd's Satisfaction

Everybody benefits when the disciples share the master's wealth at the banquet of the five thousand.

What happened on that day was repeated, as noted above, in the life of the early church. Here is Dr. Luke's description of their reaction to their new life in Christ:

> All the believers were together and had everything in common. Selling their possessions and goods, they gave to anyone as he had need. Every day they continued to meet together in the temple courts. They broke bread in their homes and ate together with glad and sincere hearts, praising God and enjoying the favor of all the people. . . . All the believers were one in heart and mind. No one claimed that any of his possessions was his own, but they shared everything they had. *With great power* the apostles continued to testify to the resurrection of the Lord (Acts 2:44-47; 4:32).

Christians relinquish the right to say "mine." Since the distinguishing mark of ownership is the owner's right to prevent anyone else from taking or using his possession, and since the Christian has acknowledged that all he is or has is God's, in reality anything that is "his" isn't his at all; he is merely managing it for God. This is contrary to our American legal system, which protects the right of ownership and finds the essence of this right in the owner's legal authority to exclude others. It's the American way, but not the Christian way.

Americans, inheritors of the Judeo-Christian ethic, commonly rely on the Ten Commandments as the source of moral scruples. Thus they believe they can be righteous by not taking what belongs to someone else ("thou shalt not steal"). Christians cannot be comfortable with this minimalist ethic, however. More is expected of them. They not only must not steal, but they must share with others what God has given them. They are to let their abundance overflow. Legalism is unsatisfactory; grace must rule.

A child may say, "That's mine," and get away with it because he is a child. An adult may say, "That's mine" and get away with it because the law of the land protects him. But the Christian who says of everything in his possession, "These are mine," cannot get away with it, since he owns nothing.

In India my wife Joy and I saw this shared Christian life in action. We stayed in the home of Leonard and Pam Thompson, Anglo-Indian ministers. It was apparent in all they did that they did not consider their house "their" home; it was a building they had rented in order to have an adequate place for their church to meet. The car they drove served the whole congregation. They didn't even consider their time their own.

We also stayed in the home of Vijai and Pushpa Lall. They occupied a large two-storied bungalow that had once housed American missionaries. We had been with them only a day when we realized that the Lalls didn't occupy the house; only one room was really theirs. All the other rooms belonged to anyone who needed a place to sleep or a meal or a meeting room for a Bible study. Their Jeep served the whole church. Not once did we hear from any of the Indian Christians, "That's mine." They had all things in common and expressed a generosity that shamed us. They also exhibited gladness in their sharing. They lived out Mahatma Gandhi's dictum: "If you have more than you need while others have less than they need, you are a thief."[10]

Jesus knew what he was talking about: "It is more blessed to give than to receive."

Contrast our Indian friends' liberality with the stinginess of King Louis XI of France. In an apparent burst of munificence, the king made a "solemn deed in covenant" to convey the entire Province of Bologne, France, to the Virgin Mary forever. A most magnanimous deed. Its splendor was somewhat diminished, however, when it was discovered that he had reserved all the revenues from the province for himself.[11] We might laugh at his hypocrisy if we weren't so aware how prone we are to proclaim publicly our total surrender to the lordship of Jesus Christ while we strive to keep all our possessions to ourselves.

We have enough abundance for gladness. If abundance has escaped us, perhaps it's because we've stifled the overflow.

One more word must be said. To whom does the overflow go?

The answer is clear. "You shall love your neighbor as yourself."

But who is my neighbor?

Who needs what you can give?

Who can ever forget that moving moment in Corrie ten Boom's *Hiding Place* when she is urgently trying to find a home for a Jewish baby. The ten Booms were Dutch Christians with a conscience. They could not bear to see their Jewish friends and neighbors suffer; they extended their concern eventually to any of the Jews who secretively knocked at their door seeking safety. Turning to a Christian pastor Corrie asks, "Would you be willing to take a Jewish mother and her baby into your home? They will almost certainly be arrested otherwise."

The pastor was aghast at the suggestion. He scolded Corrie for her involvement in the illegal concealment of the hunted Jews. Thinking it would soften his heart, Corrie showed the pastor the helpless baby. It didn't work. He stiffened himself against her pleas. "No. Definitely not. We could lose our lives for that Jewish child."

Corrie's father suddenly appeared in the doorway. "Give the child to me, Corrie," he said. He took the baby, held it close, and then looked at the pastor. "You say we could lose our lives for this child. I would consider that the greatest honor that could come to my family."

The pastor turned sharply on his heels and walked out of the room.[12]

The honor came to the ten Booms. They were arrested, condemned, and incarcerated. Father ten Boom and Corrie's sister Betsy died in the Nazi camps. Only Corrie was spared, to tell the story.

Theirs is a gripping tale of faith and courage, love and sacrifice. It contains no hint of self-pity or regret. It celebrates the abundant life and the overflow which transformed these otherwise rather ordinary Christians into courageous champions of freedom and life. They were generous. And glad because of it.

[1]Philip Yancey, ed., "Soren Kierkegaard: Desperate Measures," *Reality and the Vision.* Dallas: Word, 1990, p. 53.

[2]Francis Gay, *The Friendship Book.* London: D. C. Thomson and Co., Ltd., 1991. Thursday, March 5.

[3]See 2 Corinthians 12:10.

[4]Robert Coles, *The Spiritual Life of Children.* Boston: Houghton Mifflin, 1990, pp. 19, 20.

[5]Quoted in "Generous Folk Mentally Well," *Oregon Journal,* May 27, 1965.

[6]David Roberts, quoted by Halford Luccock, *Living Without Gloves.* New York: Oxford University, 1957, p. 39.

[7]Source unknown. Quoted in John E. Simpson, *Into My Storehouse,* New York: Revell, 1940, p. 99.

[8] *Ideas and Opinions.* New York: Bonanza Books, Crown Publishers, 1954, pp. 12, 13.

[9] Roger F. Olsen, "American Generosity Thrives in the Worst of Times," *Counsel,* published by Marts and Lundy, Inc., Summer 1991.

[10] Quoted in Simpson, *Into My Storehouse,* p. 82.

[11] Simpson, *Into My Storehouse,* p. 75.

[12] Corrie ten Boom, *The Hiding Place,* with John and Elizabeth Sherrill. Minneapolis: World Wide Pictures, Special Film Edition, pp. 112, 113.

Chapter 5

The Great "Come-as-You-Are" Party

Luke 14:1, 15-24

When a preacher talks about evangelism, veteran Christians sometimes squirm and younger Christians slink out of the room. "Soul-winners, that's what you are to be," he charges. "If every disciple of Jesus would win just one other person every year, and the next year those two would win only one more apiece, etc. etc., in a few short years the whole world would be Christian," the preacher promises. "Amen, brother, amen," say the stalwarts. The more timid in the congregation don't join in. They won't win that one. They feel they can't. They don't know how.

Evangelism isn't a popular subject even among most longtime church-goers. My guess is that it is not welcome as a discussion topic because, by and large, we preachers treat the subject too seriously. It's all challenge and duty; it requires a boldness that most people don't have. They can't see the pleasure in it.

When Jesus talks about it, though, he says pleasure is what it's all about. What you are doing is inviting people to a party, to have the time of their lives. As the dinner guest in this Scripture tells Jesus, "Blessed is the man who will eat at the feast in the kingdom of God."

In response, Jesus tells of a man who invited many guests to come to a great banquet. When the time came, however, they didn't show. Instead, they excused themselves for one fabricated reason or another. Since they couldn't come, and because he didn't want his provisions to go to waste, the host sent his servants out to bring in anybody, even the poor, crippled, blind, and lame, to eat at his table. They didn't have to be "his kind of people." They merely had to be willing to come. He was determined his food would not go to waste; he wanted guests and he wanted to bless them.

This is evangelism, pure and simple. It's telling people who are surprised to be included on the guest list that they are invited to a pretty incredible party. Evangelism isn't about Hell and judgment and escaping eternal wrath, and the evangelist isn't a duty-bound salesman with a memorized pitch to give to friend and stranger alike. We preachers like to challenge our congregations with the latest statistics proving how the rate of making Christians is falling behind the rate of population growth (which is not what the latest studies are demonstrating, by the way). Then we exhort our listeners with a variety of guilt trips to urge them to get out and win the lost. We sprinkle our exhortations with copious examples of individuals who have successfully converted the heathen to Christ. Then we take them through this or that program of four or five easy steps to salvation and urge them to get out there and try it on the unsuspecting.

It seems a thoroughly negative way to motivate them, doesn't it, especially if we're really inviting people to come to the blessing of their lives?

Let's rather become like the servant in the story, helping the host to fill the places at his table.

Whom Do You Invite?

You invite your friends. George Barna's researchers have found that on any given Sunday morning, one out of four unchurched people would willingly attend a church service if only a friend would invite them. Win Arn interviewed more than ten thousand Christians about how they came to faith in Christ and membership in churches. The results have been reported all across the land. This is why they came in the first place:

2-3% because of the church's program
5-6% because of the pastor
1-2% because they had some special needs
1-2% because someone from the church called on them
       on behalf of the church's visitation program
2-3% just "walked in"
4-5% because they liked the Sunday School
.5% because of a special crusade
75-90% because they were invited by friends or relatives.[1]

Inviting your friends to receive a blessing from God—that's evangelism.

Enlarging the circle of your friends so that more people can receive a blessing from God—that also is evangelism. Every "prospect" for the church is a prospect for a lifetime friendship. Since longtime Christians name as their best friends their brothers and sisters in Christ, by the simple process of seeking to bring others into the fellowship of the church they are enlarging their potential circle of friends.

Learning to look at other persons as prospective friends and possible future fellow Christians will change your attitude toward everyone. Much has been written lately about the polarization of America and the corresponding increase in social hostility. We've grown irritable, even dangerous. In major metropolitan areas, it has become unsafe to drive on freeways because of snipers, to venture out on city sidewalks after dark, or even to talk to strangers. Verbal sniping infects television talk shows and casual conversations. In such an atmosphere, we tend to view others as potential enemies: clerks are out to cheat us, businesses to defraud us, and neighbors to sue us.

Bob Russell, the dynamic pastor of Louisville's Southeast Christian Church, confesses a time when he succumbed to hostility. He was sitting next to a campus minister at a college basketball game when a terrible fight broke out among the players on the floor. During the brawl, one of the players grabbed a folding chair from the bench area and attempted to clobber the opposing team's players with it. Fortunately, before he could inflict too much damage the police rushed into the melee, subdued him, slapped on handcuffs and dragged him off the court. Bob thought to himself, "That is the most out-of-control human being I've ever seen. He ought to be locked up for life."

The campus minister, active in the Fellowship of Christian Athletes, didn't see an enemy. "That young man comes from the ghetto. He doesn't have much perspective about spiritual things, but I want to turn him on to the Lord so bad I can taste it."

"What a contrast," Bob mused later. "I wanted him to be locked up and this spiritual man wanted to turn him on to the Lord. What a great perspective!"[2]

That's the spirit of evangelism. You see potential friends where others see potential enemies. (Bob Russell, by the way, is one of America's great evangelists. One has to doubt that he really wanted the young man locked up. Bob's record of reaching out says otherwise.)

Our church has had excellent relationships with our "C. S. workers." These are men and women the court assigns to the church to do community service in place of doing a stretch in jail. Some of our people were a bit apprehensive at first, wondering about these "criminal types." Would our children be safe? Would our valuables be secure? Will our reputation suffer when people come onto our campus and run into workers who are so obviously not typical church members?

I'm smiling to myself in writing these words, because just last night one of our members telephoned to share some exciting news with me. He had been on a retreat with our Saturday night worship team. Over forty attended, he said, and it was an incredible experience. What made it unforgettable to him, however, was the privilege he had had of sharing Christ with Robert and later baptizing him. When Robert came up out of the water, forty men and women were standing in line to embrace and welcome him into the church family. Robert is a C.S. worker.

Or, more accurately, he *was* one. After completing his required hours of service, Robert continued to come to church (as have many other workers). This Christianity stuff was all new to him. At first, he was certain we would reject him—as certain as some of our members were that he would mock them. But what he saw and heard piqued his curiosity. He began listening to the sermons. One of our members in particular, the young man who called me last night, had impressed Robert by his friendliness and apparent concern for him. A friendship developed between them.

I should tell you that Brian did not set out to convert Robert. His motive in the beginning was to make him feel welcome at church. Brian's own background has made him sensitive to "outsiders" in church circles. He didn't come from a Christian home. To this day his family doesn't quite know what to make of him. Because he had to "break in" himself, he reaches out to others who are looking in, wondering. He reminds me of Barnabas, whose kindness made it possible for Saul of Tarsus to find acceptance in the Jerusalem church when most members were afraid of a man with his past. What began as an act of friendliness on Brian's part culminated in Robert's conversion.

John Hendee, former evangelism minister at our church and now missionary in Chile, has taught thousands of men and women how to lead others to Christ. One of the first principles he teaches is that we have to earn the right to present the gospel. First comes friendliness, then friendship, then the opening for sharing the good news about Jesus. It's what Joseph Aldrich calls "lifestyle evangelism."

To What Do You Invite Them?

You invite them to a party. Which means to something that's going to be fun for them. I know, I know—my answer does violence to the stereotype of Christians as the world's most effective killjoys.

Perhaps we get a bad press because we have a little different idea of fun from that of some people. *Partying* to Christians doesn't mean booze and broads and beds. It doesn't mean the pursuit of pleasure, either, although what we do is very pleasurable. We talk a lot more about joy than about happiness, because happiness is temporary and dependent and merely skin shallow. We want something permanent, independent of things, and deep. Drugs and drink and playing with danger aren't what make a great party for us, either. We pretty much go along with comedian Richard Pryor, who commented after his near-fatal experience with drugs, "Using drugs is the greatest feeling in the world unless you want to be a human being."

Donald Posterski puts a different spin on the same conclusion: "Living your life without God in this age is an alluring attraction unless you want to be a human being."[3]

Don't let his reference to God turn you off. We're interested in him because it is in him we find the permanent, deep, liberating life that satisfies our basic human longings. The paradox is that in turning our back on "partying" in order to get serious about life, we find that life itself becomes like a party. We discover a satisfaction and joy we hadn't known before. We can then treat even the most significant issues with a light touch.

That touch was beautifully illustrated in an article on church advertising that appeared a few years ago. "Admen for Heaven," the heading reads. It's about Tom McElligott and George Martin's partnership in producing off-the-wall advertisements to entice skeptics to give church a try. Martin is an Episcopal priest; McElligott, an ad man with the Fallon McElligott agency. Accompanying the prose is a four-picture ad, each picture having "The Episcopal Church" inscribed inconspicuously at the bottom:

The first depicts the Ten Commandments etched on two large flat stones. The caption reads, "For fast, fast, fast relief take two tablets."

The second is the portrait of England's infamous King Henry VIII. The caption: "In the church started by a man who had six wives, forgiveness goes without saying."

The third picture is of planet earth whirling through space: "Without God, it's a vicious circle."

And the fourth, my favorite, is a reproduction of Titian's masterpiece of Daniel praying in the lion's den, with this mini-sermon: "Contrary to conventional wisdom, stress is not a 20th century phenomenon."[4]

Are the ads irreverent? Perhaps, but what is more important, to an irreverent world they seem very relevant. They speak to people who seek relief from the tension in their lives, forgiveness for sins that have confused and disturbed their consciences, direction for an easily detoured life-style, and strength to stand up under the stresses that won't go away. They will catch more prospects than a good fire-breathing sermon—especially since most pre-Christians orbit a safe distance away from a preacher. These ads gently joke with the prospect, assuring him that a smile is okay in the Episcopal Church. They know that religion is more than fun and games—but they're glad to hear that fun hasn't been banished from the premises.

Who would come to a celebration where laughter was outlawed?

Why Should They Come?

You won't like my answer to this question. Why *should* they come when you invite them? They won't come because they love Jesus or fear God or are impressed with what they have heard about your church. The reason they'll accept your invitation to come to church with you or allow themselves to be influenced to take Jesus as their Savior is because of who you are.

You are their bridge or barrier to God.

Almost everyone in the Lord today is there because of some attractive person. I don't mean beautiful or handsome, but of such personality and character that their invitation was appealing.

Scary, isn't it?

Donald Posterski tells of a friend "who loves God, works hard, makes lots of money and gives an inordinate amount of what he makes to many causes." As the two of them were eating lunch one day, his friend related in his quiet way an experience with one of his business partners. The two of them had just gone through the failure of a business venture together. Their financial losses were large. Their relationship was "stressed and stretched." His partner was not a Christian.

Posterski's friend said he did what he could to be honorable throughout their ordeal, but he wasn't prepared for the Christmas gift his partner gave him. It was a book. "The content of the book is not what is important to me. But what he inscribed is what I value. I flipped open the cover and read: 'To the only person I know who gives more than he takes.'"[5]

Of all the books I have read on soul winning and church growth, I can't remember reading anywhere else of this simplest but most effective evangelistic principle: before you lay the claims of the gospel on someone, be certain you are perceived—because you are—a person who gives more than he takes. If you aren't, why should people believe you are inviting them to something that really is for their benefit and not yours?

Gail MacDonald, wife of author Gordon MacDonald, boasts about the men who run the dry cleaning business she patronizes.

The first time I went in I knew that there was something different about the place. . . . In the city you get used to being treated as if you're nothing in a lot of businesses. But then you come into this store, and you're greeted as if they'd been waiting for you all day long. I almost think I want to get something dirty so that I can have a reason to stop in there. They always have a cheerful word, despite the fact that the cleaning machinery makes the store unbearably hot and humid.

By her third visit, the operators of the business greeted her by name. They always had her cleaning ready, and it was always in excellent condition. One day she asked Larry, who works the counter, the secret of his upbeat mood, one that really made it a treat for her to do business there.

He surprised me when he said, "I'm a Christian, and I figure that that's how Christians are supposed to treat customers."[6]

Agreed, but not everyone has had Gail's experience with Christian workers. The truth remains: if they don't enjoy going into your shop, you'll never get them into your church. It's in your shop that evangelism really takes place. You are the key—not the preacher, the choir, the musicians, or the Sunday school teacher. You are the bridge or the barrier.

Robert Coles' interviews of children are almost always provocative, providing invaluable insights into their thinking, especially on spiritual matters. I read with particular interest about his work among Hopi children, since this American Indian tribe lives on a reservation in northern Arizona. He says when he first began, he met and talked with them at school, aided by a friendly principal and a cooperative teacher. The project didn't go well. After six months he was preparing to forsake the entire undertaking. The children were answering his questions, but only barely. When he asked them to make him some pictures, they drew or painted, but without enthusiasm. He recorded what he had perceived: their distrust and shyness, their cultural and social isolation, and their lack of adequate education.

A Hopi mother volunteering at the school helped to correct that perception. Robert Coles was simply not understanding. The longer you stay here," she said, "the worse it will get." Coles was surprised, confused, even angry. "I turned on her in my mind, heard myself begin to take her apart psychologically, even morally: she was officious, more than slightly self-important, a chronic busybody."

Instead of blurting out what he was feeling, though, he asked, "What do you mean?"

She told him he had failed to understand the importance of home for Hopi children.

> You see, they won't ever talk with you about the private events of their lives in this building. They learn how to read and write here; they learn their arithmetic here, but that is that. You are asking them about thoughts they put aside when they enter this building. The longer you stay here and put them in a position that forces them to appear silent and sullen and stupid, the less they'll be inclined even to answer you. Maybe they think: "This guy isn't catching!"[7]

Dr. Coles changed his technique. He went to their homes, where they could feel at ease in their natural environment. He listened when they told him about things that really mattered to them. And he learned. Not until they were convinced of his genuine interest in them would they answer his invitation to share their thoughts. Until then, it was only his party.

When Everything Is Ready, What Should You Say?

Here I depart from the text, because this is our big worry. We are afraid we won't know what to say to reach somebody. How do we speak of spiritual things? What if they ask questions we can't answer? In Jesus' parable, the great man sends his servants out to compel people to come in. It sounds so simple. When we play the role of the servants, though, we quickly conclude that we can't compel anybody to do anything. We don't have the authority to "make them come in."

Compelling isn't out of the question, however, provided that it's our invitation and not our manner that compels. When something in our words interfaces with a need in the person we're inviting, the result is an invitation too enticing to be rejected.

That something, of course, is a word of testimony about what you, the inviting servant, have already received—and how much good they will receive as well. Nothing sells like a satisfied customer. No one persuades like a persuaded speaker.

Because I speak all the time to the same congregation, I don't give my own simple testimony very often. In a sermon just a couple of weeks ago, however, I spoke rather feelingly of my basic belief in God, and when I later offered the invitation for persons to accept Christ as Lord and Savior, the response was what you would expect at the climax of a revival meeting. Several respondents later told me they were persuaded by my simple statement of belief.

E. Stanley Jones, the famous missionary to India of a couple generations ago, wrote in his autobiography of a similar experience. It happened not long after he received his call to the ministry. He shared his good news with his pastor, who surprised the young man by asking him to preach on an upcoming Sunday night. Jones said he prepared thoroughly, wanting to make a good impression and to "argue his case acceptably." When the evening came, a large crowd assembled, full of expectancy. They wanted to encourage the novice.

He began "on rather a high key," he said, but hadn't completed more than a half dozen sentences when out came a word he had never used before—or since. *Indifferentism.* As soon as he had uttered it, he spotted a college girl putting her head down and smiling. It so upset him that he lost the thread of his discourse and couldn't find it again. He stood before the assembled throng without a word to say.

> I do not know how long I stood there rubbing my hands hoping that something would come back. It seemed an age. Finally I blurted out, "Friends, I am very sorry, but I have forgotten my sermon." I started down the steps leading from the pulpit in shame and confusion. This was the beginning of my ministry, I thought—a tragic failure. As I was about to leave the pulpit a Voice seemed to say to me, "Haven't I done anything for you?"
> "Yes," I replied. "You have done everything for me."
> "Well," answered the Voice, "couldn't you tell that?"
> "Yes, I suppose I could," I eagerly replied.

Jones turned around, walked to the front of the pulpit on the main floor, and spoke very simply.

> Friends, I see I cannot preach, but I love Jesus Christ. You know what my life was in this community—that of a wild, reckless young man—and you know what it now is. You know he has made life new for me, and though I cannot preach I am determined to love and serve him.

At the close of the service a boy came up and said, "Stanley, I wish I could find what you have found."[8] And he did. Stanley Jones did no more than tell his story. It was enough.

Evangelism, as Dr. Jones discovered so early in his career, is what D. T. Niles calls it, "an overflow of the church's life, not a mere program of activities."[9] That life is measured not by the variety or number or quality of the church's programs, but by the testimony of changed lives lived honestly and lovingly before God and people.

Nobody has made this clearer than Rufus Jones, who insists that religion "is a divine spring and capacity which belongs to our being as men. Religion is just overbrimming, abounding life." It is what we mean when we exult, "My cup runneth over."

Salvation, which is ultimately what the invitation is about, is the attainment of complete normal spiritual health. As Phillips Brooks used to say,

> The cool, calm vigor of the normal human life; the making of the man to be himself; the calling up out of the depth of his being and the filling with vitality of that self which is truly he—that is salvation.

Rufus Jones helpfully adds that "the task of religion is not like that of laboriously endeavoring to teach an elephant to fly; it is rather the discovery of the potential capacities for flight in a being that was framed for the upper air."[10]

When we invite men and women to the Lord's Party, we are inviting them to enter the environment for which they were created, to fly as they were intended to fly, to be at home with God, where they belong and where they can be their best selves.

---

[1]Win Arn, Charles Arn, *The Master's Plan for Making Disciples,* Pasadena: Church Growth Press, 1982, p. 43.

[2]Bob Russell, *Take Comfort.* Cincinnati: Standard Publishing Company, 1991, pp. 101, 102.

[3]Donald C. Posterski, *Reinventing Evangelism.* Downers Grove: InterVarsity, 1989, p. 95.

[4]"Admen for Heaven," *Christianity Today,* September 18, 1987, pp. 12, 13.

[5]Posterski, *Reinventing Evangelism,* p. 26.

[6]Gordon MacDonald, *Christ Followers in the Real World.* Nashville: Oliver Nelson, 1991, p. 203. Used by permission.

[7]Robert Coles, *The Spiritual Life of Children.* Boston: Houghton, Mifflin Company, 1990, p. 24.

[8]E. Stanley Jones, *The Christ of the Indian Road.* Nashville: Abingdon, 1925, pp. 149, 150. Copyright renewal ©1953 by E. Stanley Jones. Excerpted by permission of the publisher, Abingdon Press.

[9]D. T. Niles, *That They May Have Life.* New York: Harper, 1951, p. 78.

[10]*Rufus Jones Speaks to Our Time,* ed. Harry Emerson Fosdick. New York: Macmillan, 1951, p. 65.

Chapter 6

When You're Tired of Pigging Out

Luke 15:11-32

"Why does this make me uncomfortable? I agree with almost everything being said." My friend and I were sitting with our wives high up in the arena at a national Christian conference. His whispered discomfort surprised me. I had been thinking the same thing to myself, but I was fairly certain I was the only one in the room who was squirming. Each time the speaker would roar away at another rhetorical target, the audience would roar back in applause. My colleague and I were out of step with this crowd, even though many of our convictions agreed with the speaker's.

My disquiet was all the more unnerving because the speakers are my friends. They are committed Christians, hard-working and compassionate, eager to serve Christ and to save every sinner they can reach. But when their voices filled the arena, they didn't resonate with sympathy for the lost but with righteous indignation and harsh judgment. And the largely homogeneous crowd heard them gladly.

Singled out for condemnation were homosexuals, divorced persons, women in church leadership positions and the liberal churches who put them there, women who have had abortions and anyone who sympathizes with them, all political liberals and the agencies who agree with them, and many, many others.

I thought of some of my former students and a few church members who have struggled with their sexual identity. Some have left their homosexual practices, others have left the church, and still others continue their agonizing. They would have heard no word of hope here. There was no good news for them.

I thought of a desperate young woman who resorted to abortion because she was convinced she had no alternative. She felt trapped. She hoped God could forgive her. She could hardly forgive herself. Was there any word from the Lord for her here?

I tried to put myself mentally in the seat of each person the speakers scorned and wondered whether anything would be said to give a person like me, already ashamed of my actions, any reason to believe I could find a home in a church, a savior in Jesus. Instead of being drawn to the love of God, all of my various persona just wanted out, away from the preaching pointed so fiercely at them, away from the condemners to the sympathetic condemned.

But I could find no solace in the fact that *they* were condemning and I was not. I have taken my turn at the same exercise. On many occasions I too have donned my Pharisee's robe to fulminate against this or that social evil (and its perpetrators) from my loft of supposed innocence. Jesus' defense of sinners very much like the ones being regularly flayed at this conclave came to mind. Much to the disgust of the "Pharisees and the teachers of the law who belonged to their sect, he was eating at the banquet Levi the tax collector hosted in his honor." They voiced their disdain to his disciples. "Why do you eat and drink with tax collectors and 'sinners'?" Levi had invited many of his friends to the banquet and, as you would expect, many of them were fellow tax collectors. Not many respectable people would consort with these social pariahs.

Jesus overheard their grumbling and replied, "It is not the healthy who need a doctor, but the sick. I have not come to call the righteous, but sinners to repentance" (Luke 5:27-32). His method wasn't to preach at them but to eat with them. ("You catch more flies with honey than with vinegar," my father used to tell me.)

So there we were, my uncomfortable friend and I, being bombarded by preaching directed to the saved against the sinners, while the audience clapped *for* the speakers and *against* the sinners. That night I vowed to examine my own preaching with greater scrupulousness than I ever had done before and to remind myself, with each new homiletical attempt I make, that the gospel was, is, and always must be Good News to the sinner.

Jesus' parable of the tax collector and the Pharisee came to mind.

> To some *who were confident of their own righteousness and looked down on everybody else,* Jesus told this parable: Two men went up to the temple to pray, one a Pharisee and the other a tax collector. The Pharisee stood up and prayed about himself: "God, I thank you that I am not like other men—robbers, evildoers, adulterers—or even like this tax collector. I fast twice a week and give a tenth of all I get."
>
> But the tax collector stood at a distance. He would not even look up to heaven, but beat his breast and said, "God, have mercy on me, a sinner" (Luke 18:9-13).

I also remembered Jesus' startling application of his simple story. And I squirmed even more.

> I tell you that this man, rather than the other, went home justified before God. For everyone who exalts himself will be humbled, and he who humbles himself will be exalted.

The Scriptures wouldn't leave me alone, wouldn't let me justify either the speakers or myself.

And then I thought of the prodigal son's elder brother, so certain of his righteousness, so jealous of his brother, so out of step with his father.

Even though I readily forget, I shouldn't, because all my life I have clung for dear life to this parable about the faithful father, the two brothers, and their three parties. Since I'm an ordained preacher, you might place me in the role of the pious older brother, but I have always identified more with the prodigal son, the headstrong young man who thought he was ready to be on his own, out from under his father's watchful eye, who had songs to sing and women to woo and sins to commit. As far as he was concerned, life should be a party. More than a party, even. A pig-out.

A Pig-out

He may have been of age, but as a colleague once said of Prime Minister Gladstone of England, he was "a wonderful man and full of boy." He was more boy than man at this stage, filled with wonder, wanting it all, believing he deserved it, ready to do everything his way.

He must have been something like the nineteenth-century Algernon Swinburne, who devoted himself passionately to his bohemian life-style. He ate and drank and made merry, scorning the Christianity of his day as too cranky, too confining for free spirits like his. He, too, wanted it all. Yet his sensuous pig-out wasn't entirely satisfying, either, as he complained after one too many a hangover:

> From too much love of living,
> From hope and fear set free,
> We thank with brief thanksgiving
> Whatever gods may be
> That no life lives forever;
> That dead men rise up never;
> That even the weariest river
> Winds somewhere safe to sea.[1]

Swinburne sounds like a man who has finally sobered up, like the prodigal son who at last "came to his senses." But in Swinburne's case, there was no loving father to return to. Just death, from which there is no waking. I have done my share of preaching against the Swinburnes of this world and their wild, reckless partying. I haven't reached them. I wouldn't have reached the young Algernon, either. Even when the party was over, he wouldn't have turned for safety to a crank like me.

Jesus' method was better than mine. Instead of condemning their thirst he offered them a better drink. Once, for example, at the Feast of Tabernacles in Jerusalem, when people were celebrating God's miraculous deliverance from Israel's bondage in Egypt with their usual mixture of pious ritual and happy socializing, laughing and eating and drinking and thoroughly enjoying themselves, Jesus stood up and in a loud voice invited them to himself. "If anyone is thirsty, let him come to me and drink. Whoever believes in me, as the Scripture has said, streams of living water will flow from within him" (John 7:37, 38).

No condemnation of their reliance on religious ritual or their probable excesses in celebration. Neither of these—just an offer of something better.

A Homecoming Party

The prodigal son also was ready for something better. That's the reason he returned home. He came to his senses, or, as the RSV puts it, "he came to himself." The pig-out was over; sobriety had returned.

John Killinger says probably "the best thing you can ever do for God is to be yourself." It sounds easy, but it isn't. In fact, he says,

> We have acquired the notion somewhere that we cannot afford to be honest, to be who we are, and that we must always take care to project some other image, the one we think others—and God—would expect of us. We spend our lives hiding our real selves and putting forward our fabricated selves, our doctored alter-egos, our polite and respectable doubles.[2]

We don't want to be found out, so we camouflage our-selves.

But we can't do it indefinitely. We slip up, the real person slips out, and we're caught red-handed trying to be something or somebody else. Then we have only a couple of choices: we can push ahead, brazenly pretending but fooling no one, or we can try to return to the beginning, to what Clovis Chappel calls the "land of beginning again."

> I wish that there were some wonderful place
> Called the Land of Beginning Again,
>> Where all our mistakes and all our heartaches,
> And all our poor selfish grief
>> Could be dropped like a shabby old coat at the door.
> And never be put on again.[3]

Something like that happened to the prodigal son. He went home, and his father put a new coat on him. He began to live again.

He had returned to his origins.

Isaiah also urges a return to the land of beginning again, in this instance called "the rock from which you were cut":

> Listen to me, you who pursue righteousness
>> and who seek the Lord:
> Look to the rock from which you were cut
>> and to the quarry from which you were hewn;
> look to Abraham, your father,
>> and to Sarah, who gave you birth.
> When I called him he was but one,
>> and I blessed him and made him many.
> The Lord will surely comfort Zion
>> and will look with compassion on all her ruins;
> he will make her deserts like Eden,
>> her wastelands like the garden of the Lord.
> Joy and gladness will be found in her,
>> thanksgiving and the sound of singing (Isaiah 51:1-3).

In the parable the father is like God. No other scriptural picture of him has been more helpful to me. The profundities of the theologians often confuse or mystify, but this often errant child can believe in a God who waits like this father for his wandering son to come home, to begin again. He obviously loves his prodigal son as much as his pious one. He greets him with compassion. A less God-like parent could not have resisted the opportunity to spit out the long-stifled scolding the son so richly deserves.

Mrs. Billy Graham seems the epitome of sanctity to most Americans. Wife of America's most famous evangelist, daughter of the prominent Dr. Nelson Bell, missionary to China, Ruth Graham has led a nearly ideal life. Yet when she was very small, her parents entrusted her to the hands of an *amah* (nanny) whose unsavory past would have disqualified her for the job, except for one thing: she had found the land of beginning again.

Wang Nai-Nai (pronounced "nanny," the word means "old lady") had been a procuress, a vile occupation. She and her husband had run a traffic in small girls. They bought some from impoverished parents and kidnapped others to sell to Shanghai for teahouses as "little flowers," young prostitutes. It's hard to imagine a meaner career than stealing little girls to make prostitutes out of them. Inhuman.

One day, however, this heartless woman overheard singing from a little gospel hall in Tsingkiangpu. Intrigued, she entered, listened to someone talking about Christ, and gave herself to him at once. She wasn't yet a church member when she joined the Bells' service, but she became one shortly. Still illiterate, she saved stubs of candles and late at night she'd lie on the floor in front of the fireplace, learning to read by candlelight. Like Mary Magdalene, she never forgot.

As a small child entrusted to her care, Ruth knew nothing of her background, but years later she could remember her sitting on a little stool, with her battered

Bible and hymn book, singing the Chinese translation of Cowper's "There Is a Fountain Filled With Blood," especially the lines:

> The dying thief rejoiced to see
> That fountain in his day;
> And there may I, though vile as he,
> Wash all my sins away.[4]

Wang Nai-Nai, Mary Magdalene, Zaccheus the tax collector, Saul the persecutor, the thief on the cross, the thieves in the Ephesian church (Ephesians 4:28), and all other kinds of sinner, when they come to themselves, can return to the land of beginning again where a loving Father waits to throw a welcome home party for them.

A Pity Party

Not everybody is celebrating the prodigal's return, however. The older brother, smug in his sanctimony, won't attend the party. His own pity party claims all his attention.

> Look! All these years I've been slaving for you and never disobeyed your orders. Yet you never gave me even a young goat so I could celebrate with my friends. But when this son of yours who has squandered your property with prostitutes comes home, you kill the fattened calf for him!

Such unfairness. What a pity!

John Ortberg tells a tale of two other brothers, brothers in Christ. Ned, who attended the same church for more than four decades, was "a crabby little kid" who grew into a crabby young man and, after his religious conversion, "became a crabby Christian."

> He gives no evidence of uncertainty in his faith. He believes the Bible from cover to cover, and he believes the cover is genuine leather. But there doesn't seem to be any record

over the last forty years of Ned's ever changing his disposition, his mind, his expression, or his pew.

He complained of the lack of commitment in today's young people and boasted of his own daily devotional habits. "But Ned," said Ortberg,

> You're still crabby. You've crabbed your way through 14,200 quiet times without changing. What's the point of doing all this religious activity and still being the crabgrass in the ecclesiastical lawn?

Ned's brother in Christ, Harold, on the other hand, had done it all wrong. He'd messed up his marriage, messed with drugs, and ended up without a job. His multiplied disaster drove him to church. He didn't go in very far at first, only as far as the back row.

But he came back the next week, carrying a Bible. He started getting up at 4:00 A.M. to read it. In a few months, he accepted Christ as Lord and Savior, was baptized, joined a small group, and began serving.

Harold's life changed so abruptly Ortberg wondered whether the change would last. But now, several years later, his wife, his children, his friends, and Harold himself agree that he is a new man.[5]

John Ortberg admits, "It is probably unrealistic to expect all conversion stories to be as dramatic as Harold's. One kiss does not always turn the frog into a prince. But shouldn't we at least be producing kinder, gentler frogs?"

This is the older brother's problem, isn't it? He was right in his convictions and right in his practice, but wrong in his attitude. The speakers in that long-ago convention I attended were also correct. Like my friend, I agreed with much of what I was hearing, but winced at the tone of voice and the implied condemnation. It just didn't square with the character of the prodigal son's father.

Long ago Aristotle counseled moderation in all things. Would he have included spiritual virtues among "all things"? He would probably have listed at least some of them.

"If practiced to perfection," the philosopher opined, "any virtue can become a vice. Prudence creates niggardliness; honesty, cruelty; self-respect, vainglory; knowledge, condescension; justice, heartlessness; temperance, aridity; chastity, barrenness." Forrester Church, commenting on Aristotle's counsel, notes,

> There is no virtue that is not potentially an idol capable of reducing its worshipers to abject solemnity. Which is why the angels are so chary of perfectionism.[6]

That sounds perfectly rational, yet didn't Jesus urge us to be perfect as our heavenly father is perfect? What's a believer to do?

Jesus didn't condemn the Pharisees' religious practices because he thought they were practicing some degenerate form of religion. They were religion's best. They were punctilious in their observance of their rituals and super-conscientious in matters of morality. It was their air of superiority, not their inferiority, that caused Jesus to point out the flaws of their Pharisaism. These religiously righteous souls knew the Scriptures, obeyed their commands, tithed and double-tithed their income, were faithful in prayer and devoted to their faith. Any church would boast of their Christian equivalents today. Why, then, did Jesus criticize them so?

He wasn't criticizing them *per se*. They were symbols of something dangerous, and that is religion itself, or at least religion that is reduced to rites and laws and special observances and categories of judgment. When your form of religion encourages self-congratulation because of your spiritual achievements and condemnation of others for behavior unbefitting your moral and spiritual code of conduct, it severs you from humanity and distances you from the Father of this world's prodigals. When you then discover God welcoming and throwing parties for the very persons you have ostracized, the criticism you formerly aimed at them you turn on God. As James D. Smart has astutely observed,

> Every form of religion has in it the danger of becoming not a highway to God but rather an obstacle between man and God blocking the highway on which God seeks to come to man.[7]

The problem is not with *religion,* but with the *religious.* Always insecure, we seek to bolster our sagging spirits by focusing on the measurable, categorical elements of the faith. We reserve judgment, naturally, for the easily observable sins. I may be able to hide my greed, pride, doubt, lack of love, racism, sexism, and meanness of spirit from most people most of the time, but I can flaunt my attendance at worship services, my tithing, my service on committees, and my many memorized Scriptures. At the same time, I can be quick to point with horror to the divorcee, the abortionist, the homosexual, and other persons so flagrantly in violation of my religion's mores.

Unless I'm careful, I can fall into the trap that caught the two ladies who praised Dr. Samuel Johnson, when his *Dictionary of the English Language* made him famous in his own time, for using no filthy words. The learned gentleman answered in mock surprise: "What, my dears? Then you have been looking for them!"

Perhaps the best symbol for this scavenging bent of mind besides Jesus' "whited sepulchres" is one found in June Singer's *Boundaries of the Soul.* The author describes a most proper young woman who came to see her for psychoanalysis. The conservative patient recounted a vivid dream in which she visited her analyst's office attired in a black velvet gown with a high neck and long sleeves. She was beautiful and proper. So she seemed until she turned around; in back she was naked from top to bottom. On days when I have veered too close to denunciation in the pulpit, I've remembered that image and pictured myself turning to leave and granting the congregation too candid a shot of the real me. One whose own guilt is so scantily covered had best not venture into condemning another. I can pile layers of clothes over my sinfulness, but I cannot deny it is there.

Dorothy Sayers captures the essence of our fraternity with other sinners in one of her radio plays. The setting is the Zebedees' house in Jerusalem an hour before dawn on the first day of the week after Jesus died on the previous Friday—betrayed by Judas, denied by Peter. Someone knocks softly at the door. John answers and finds Mary Magdalene standing there. He invites her in. She asks whether Peter is with John. "He is," John says.

> Like a sick animal that has crawled home to die. He can't eat. He can't sleep. He can't forgive himself. It was my fault. I knew he was frightened, yet I left him alone in the house of Annas. Dear Lord! was there none of us you could trust for five minutes?
>
> *Mary:* Poor Peter. He takes his failures hard.
> *John:* He calls himself a worse traitor than. . . . I can't speak the name. I can't say our Master's prayer. "Forgive us our trespasses as we forgive"—no, it's impossible. . . . You heard what became of him?
> *Mary:* Yes. John, you can't hate him worse than he came to hate himself. His self-hatred murdered him.
> *John* (slowly): If I hate him, I am his murderer too. . . . O God! there is no end to our sins! Do we all murder Jesus and one another?[8]

Yes, John, we do. And that is the reason, that night, high up in the arena, I was squirming. If only I could have convinced myself that I had conquered my own sinfulness, that I really had become like Christ, I could have heard the prophetic thunderations more gladly. If only I were more like Christ and less like Peter. If only more like the father in Jesus' story and less like the brothers.

That's right—like the *brothers,* both of them, for whenever I imagine myself in the drama, I play both roles. By profession, I am the older brother, professionally righteous, ordained to religious leadership, dutiful in observing the ecclesiastical functions of my office and in rising to the expectations imposed on the clergy. By character, I am the younger brother, restless when confined, rebellious when ordered, insatiably hungry for this world's best, and indifferent to the consequences of my own lusts. If God isn't patient with the likes of both brothers, there's no hope for the likes of me.

C. S. Lewis helps here, as he does so often, with his reminder that

> Christianity will do you good—a great deal more good than you ever wanted or expected. And the first bit of good it will do you is to hammer into your head (you won't enjoy that!) the fact that what you have hitherto called "good"—all that about "leading a decent life" and "being kind"—isn't quite the magnificent and all-important affair you supposed. It will teach you that in fact you can't be "good" (not for twenty-four hours) on your own moral effort. And then it will teach you that even if you were, you still wouldn't have achieved the purpose for which you were created. Mere morality is not the end of life. You were made for something quite different from that. . . .

What surprising language, to speak of morality as "mere." What is the "something quite different" that can surpass a decent life?

Lewis admits later that morality is indispensable, but it will be swallowed up when we are re-made.

> All the rabbit in us is to disappear—the worried, conscientious, ethical rabbit as well as the cowardly and sensual rabbit. We shall bleed and squeal as the handfuls of fur

come out; and then, surprisingly, we shall find underneath it all a thing we have never yet imagined: a real Man, an ageless god, a son of God, strong, radiant, wise, beautiful, and drenched in joy.[9]

And then we really celebrate. All of us, younger and older brothers (and sisters) alike, can celebrate. What a party it will be!

[1]Cited in Ralph W. Sockman, *The Higher Happiness.* Nashville: Abingdon-Cokesbury, 1950, p. 51.

[2]*For God's Sake Be Human.* Waco: Word, 1970, p. 17.

[3]Clovis G. Chappel, *Meet These Men,* p. 59.

[4]John C. Pollock, *A Foreign Devil in China.* Grand Rapids: Zondervan, 1971, p. 83.

[5]John Ortberg, Jr., "What Changes at Conversion?" *Leadership* Magazine, Summer 1991, pp. 52, 53.

[6]F. Forrester Church in *Entertaining Angels,* quoted in *Christianity Today,* October 21, 1988, p. 33.

[7]James D. Smart, *The ABC's of Christian Faith.* Philadelphia: Westminster Press, 1968, p. 27.

[8]Dorothy L. Sayers, "The King Comes to His Own," *The Man Born to Be King.* London: Victor Gollancz, Ltd., 1944, pp. 323, 324. Used by permission of Ignatius Press, London.

[9]C. S. Lewis, *The Business of Heaven,* ed. Walter Hooper. Great Britain: Collins, 1984, pp. 296, 297.

Chapter 7

When You Care Enough
to Give the Very Best

John 12:1-8

It was a bittersweet affair, this farewell party in Bethany. So severe had the pressure against Jesus become, he could no longer move about publicly. He and his disciples had been in seclusion in the village of Ephraim, near the Judean desert, but now it was time for the Passover, Jesus' moment of destiny. The small band left their retreat and headed for the city, stopping en route to visit Jesus' friends Lazarus and Mary and Martha in the Jerusalem suburb of Bethany. Any visit from Jesus was cause for rejoicing among these good friends, but this one was even more so. It was his first return since he had miraculously summoned Lazarus from his tomb. The family prepared a dinner in Jesus' honor, with Lazarus in attendance as proof of the Lord's power. What an evening of jubilation it must have been.

No, *jubilation* is too exuberant a word for this occasion. Thanksgiving and congratulating and exulting in each other's company were in abundance, of course, at least at first. But I suspect that whenever the conversation lagged, every mind reverted to thoughts of the danger Jesus was in. Jerusalem was abuzz with rumors of what the chief priests and elders would do if they could get their hands on the mischief maker. They had already issued orders that "if anyone found out where Jesus was, he should report it so that they might arrest him" (John

11:57). His disciples had tried to dissuade him from going to Jerusalem at all, even when they had learned of Lazarus' death. When Thomas sensed the Master's determination to go in spite of everything, he resigned himself to the inevitable. "Let us also go," he said to the others, "that we may die with him" (John 11:16).

So an air of foreboding permeated the group that evening. Not all parties are hilarious. Some, like this one, are quietly sad: the joy of friends reuniting mingled with the sadness of impending separation. These are unforgettable events in one's life. Expressing the inexpressible, they celebrate the ties that bind; they are, as I said, bittersweet.

The friends' pain would have been eased if only they had known that the events of the next few days would end in triumph and not tragedy. Even though Jesus had repeatedly prepared his friends for his death and resurrection, they hadn't comprehended his meaning. Death they knew something about; resurrection remained a puzzle, even after Lazarus had returned from death.

When our Scandinavian tour group said good-byes at the airport, we struggled to find the right words to say. Some of us had traveled together before; for others, this was a first. When twenty-five compatible persons live together for fifteen days, they can grow remarkably close. Farewells are not easy. After visiting Copenhagen, Stockholm, the Norwegian fjord country, Bergen and Oslo, we flew back to Amsterdam, where we split up, flying to our respective American ports of entry in Minneapolis, Detroit, Chicago, and Los Angeles. Sandy Zacharias, veteran of an earlier tour to Israel, told us she found this parting easier than last time. "Then," she said, "I thought I wouldn't be seeing any of you again. It was hard to say good-bye." But when we held a reunion of the group in Arizona several months later, Sandy was there. Since we were already planning this tour's reunion, and Sandy was planning to attend, she could say, "This time I know I'll be seeing you again, so it's easier."

The diners at Martha's table weren't so certain of their future. What exactly lay in store for their friend Jesus? Once he entered Jerusalem, would they ever see him again?

Was Mary asking such questions as she took up the precious balm to anoint Jesus? What intuition drove her to her act of consecration, one so remarkable the story— or a similar one—is told in each of the four Gospels. The story varies considerably in the telling. In Mark 14:3-9, an unnamed woman anoints the head (not the feet) of Jesus; in Luke 7:36-38 a "sinful woman" comes with an alabaster jar of ointment, but her copious tears first wet Jesus' feet, which she then wipes with her hair and anoints with the ointment. Matthew and Mark name the host Simon the Leper, Luke calls him one of the Pharisees, and John implies that Jesus' friends Lazarus, Mary, and Martha had opened their home for the occasion. Bible scholars wonder whether these are four tellings of the same incident, each remembered a little differently by the teller, or two incidents that became mixed in the narrating through time, one incident concerning the sinful woman whose hair wiped her tears from Jesus' feet and the other concerning one who brought expensive perfumed nard.

There are variations, but there are also constants: Jesus at the center of the story, appreciating the kindness done him; a woman who ministers to him in humble love, heedless of cost or criticism; and strong disapproval of her wastefulness.

Jesus promised that the woman's tender act would never be forgotten. "I tell you the truth, wherever this gospel is preached throughout the world, what she has done will also be told, in memory of her" (Matthew 26:13; Mark 14:9). Though Jesus was a prophet, prophetic insight wasn't required to make this forecast. Moments like this one are unforgettable. The episode combines the elements of high drama: the players act in anticipation of a tragic miscarriage of justice. Their hero faces the crisis of his career. The woman acts on behalf of all his friends to symbolize their devotion to him. Later, whenever they would reminisce about their days with him, they would remember the ache, the danger, the communion of their souls as they reclined at the table. They would never forget and never tire of talking about it.

They would be like veterans of war who fought and feared together and experienced an intensity in life they would relish ever afterwards. When senior citizens in London a few years ago were asked, for example, to name the happiest time of their lives, sixty percent answered, "The Blitz." Think of it. Night after incessant night for what seemed an endless stretch of horror the *Luftwaffe* bombers dumped demolition on the city. Rubble lay where once proud architecture reigned. People burrowed like gophers into their hiding places and prayed for deliverance. It was a black hour for Britain. Now these same victims remembered, and were glad they had been there, when they had lived deep.

They would be telling it ages hence, these guests in Bethany. In those final hours before the passion of Jesus, they lived deep. And when they told of it in years to come, they would always highlight the woman, the criticism, and the Savior.

So shall we.

The Spendthrift

We begin with the woman. According to John, she is Mary, one of Jesus' best friends. We can understand, then, the liberties she takes in anointing his feet (surprising in itself) and in unbinding her hair, something a proper Jewish woman would seldom do in mixed company. Even her "squandering" of the expensive perfume makes sense, doesn't it? How does the cost compare with the gift Jesus had already given her and Martha, their brother back from the grave? When the purpose of the party is to say thanks, who can withhold an extravagance?

104

What we already know about Mary also lends credence to John's account. We met her in Luke 10:38-42, on an earlier visit of Jesus. The two sisters hosted Jesus, each in her own way. Martha, the practical one, the good homemaker, bustled about with cleaning and cooking and making certain everything was in order and on time for the meal. She resented her sister, who was ignoring the preparations as she drank in Jesus' every word. Mary was also being hospitable, though. Giving Jesus her undivided attention, she sat at his feet, encouraging him to keep on speaking. To the Marthas of this world, the "practical" ones, Mary seems impractical or, even worse, irresponsible.

She reminds me of some other sanguine personalities I have known. We tease my administrative assistant, Judy, as the Mary of our staff—buoyant, always ready for a party, willing to do anything so long as she can make it fun. But in all fairness, Judy is really as practical as Martha, too. We razz the Mary in her because—well, because Marys can take a kidding. Marthas are sometimes a little uptight. They have too much serious work to do, and are in too much of a hurry to get it done, to tolerate much teasing.

This story is about Mary. Martha just couldn't have lavished so much of the perfume even if she had wanted to, which I suspect she might have. She might have longed, for once in her life, to do something out of character, to be boldly, even foolishly, generous, spontaneous, out of control with gratitude and love for the Lord. But she couldn't. She must be practical.

Don't castigate her, though. She is no less into this party than Mary. It is she, remember, who is making the preparations for the meal. Without Marthas, there'd be no parties for the Marys to shine in.

Both Martha and Mary fill the house with the incense of their praise. Martha's comes from the kitchen and table, the aroma of tantalizing victuals offered with love, and Mary's from the excess of nard poured on

Jesus' feet and spread with her unbound hair. Not going as far as Mary (whose gift was worth a year of a man's hard labor), Martha surely overspent the grocery budget to do Jesus justice. The Lord was blessed by both of them.

Mary's is the more unexpected gift. She pours out her expensive gift on him—which is, by the way, what good friends do, isn't it? Can you have a really good friend with whom you are not generous? Friendship and generosity go together, don't they? If you are unable ever to squander your goods on somebody, you're probably not capable of a close friendship. A good friend is a spendthrift, where you are concerned.

The Spoilsport

There seems to be one at every party, doesn't there? The man or woman determined not to have a good time and, if possible, to prevent everybody else from having one. Negative, critical, and selfish, he is the elder brother at the prodigal son's return, the jealous Cain slaying Abel, the Diotrephes who must be first[1], the Judas who covets other people's money.

Judas, too, is at this party, but not of it. He keeps his distance, sternly withholding himself from the spirit of the moment. He misreads his Lord. Astutely aware of Jesus' love of the poor, he appeals to a lofty principle to make his low-down point. Insensitive to the woman, he denigrates her gift and openly condemns her generosity. He sounds like a champion of the poor, but John isn't fooled.

"He did not say this because he cared about the poor but because he was a thief; as keeper of the money bag, he used to help himself to what was put into it" (John 12:6).

The truth is, Judas is the champion of no one but himself, at least as John portrays him. He is the typical spoilsport, unable to have any fun at the party because he can't forget himself.

It is not only the fun he misses. He misses also the pain. The wrench of parting will not be his. He hasn't "bonded" with anyone, even Jesus. His relationship with Jesus is a utilitarian one; he has signed on with the Messiah for purposes of his own. He may have looked upon the Master as a revolutionary, one who could rally Israel to throw off the yoke of Rome and establish Jewish freedom. But if he did, he does no more. Jesus is in trouble. And his encouragement of this foolishness of Mary's is one reason why. He isn't tough enough; he lacks single-mindedness.

So Judas can't join in the laughter, and he can't feel the sentiment of the evening. His is a failure of sympathy. He remains, as all dedicated critics do, the outsider. He misses the power of the human drama being played before him. His eye, instead, is on the money. She is squandering funds that should have been put into the ministry. (Or, as John discloses, into Judas's pockets).

He is twice a thief. He steals people's money; he also steals their pleasure. It really wasn't Judas's business anyway what Mary did with her gift, or what Jesus felt about her giving it. What demons drove him to spoil their moment?

Victor Borge tells a delightful story of another spoiler. Maestro Leopold Stokowski was conducting the Philadelphia Orchestra in the *Leonore Overture Number Three*. The score calls for an offstage trumpet call to be sounded at two intervals. Both times Stokowski's baton signaled, but no sound answered. Not known for his long-suffering demeanor, Stokowski rushed into the wings as soon as he could, ready to blister his delinquent trumpet player for missing his cue. When he got there, he found the player eager to blow his bit, but unable. He was still struggling in the arms of a burly watchman. "I tell you," the dutiful guard said, "you can't blow that __ thing in here. There's a concert going on!"[2]

Going the watchman one better, Judas would not only have restrained the trumpet player but prevented the whole concert unless he could conduct. And Mary's adulation of Jesus, an appreciation Judas may once have felt but felt no more, was intolerable. As events in the next few hours would prove, Jesus was a hero to Judas no longer.

But then, no one else was, either. One who steals money and pleasure steals praise as well. He has no heroes, and he'll tolerate no hero worship if he can help it. Many pundits have written on the absence of heroes in our time. Pining back to the days of Eisenhower and Churchill and even Kennedy, these writers note correctly that there are no such giants in our day. Few of them seem to connect that observation with another one equally true: we have not because we desire not. We can't make ourselves Number One and have any hero beyond ourselves. "In the end," Amitai Etzioni, a professor of government has observed, "we can't stomach a real hero. We're happy to have heroes for a week, but we have to tear them down."[3]

Thus Judas.

The Grateful Recipient

Wouldn't you have expected Jesus to side with Judas, even though the disciple's motives weren't as pure as you might wish? Don't you find Jesus' words just a little surprising? "Leave her alone." But she is, in fact, laying waste a small fortune here. The disciples have so little money for their work, and there are so many needs. Anyone who has been in Christian work can sympathize with Judas, can feel so keenly the need for resources for ministry that the sentiment of Judas is one often felt. Who hasn't said, when a rival organization falls heir to a legacy, "Why them, Lord, and not us?" Who hasn't observed the extravagant life-styles of some Christians and muttered about how much more money would be available to charitable works like ours if believers would only cut back to a simpler way of life and donate the difference?

What discourages me about this episode is my awareness that of the three major personalities portrayed
here, the one I'm most like is Judas. You see, I am a minister with a dynamic church that's always broke, and in
recent years I've been trying to help a college that has
been in even worse financial condition. If I had seen
Mary wasting that precious asset, I'd likely have thought
of budget deficits and cried out as Judas did.

When I read recently that a baseball player had signed
a six-year contract for $42,000,000, the Judas in me had
to fight resentment. Think how many of the poor could
be helped by that one man's salary!

Judas's speech is mine. "Think how many other people you could help with what you are wasting! How can
you in good conscious squander all that precious ointment when there are such enormous needs in the kingdom of God?" I don't like myself when I sound like the
disciples' treasurer, but the truth is I have made his
speech.

Given my experience and that of many other Christian
workers, I'd have to say that Judas's words are right
even if his heart isn't. He seems to be looking out for the
interests of others. John knows better. He doesn't let
Judas off the hook; he characterizes him as a selfish,
grasping man, a thief—certainly a spoilsport.

The scale of values Judas espouses seems so sensible
that the dedicated reader is somewhat surprised, even
offended, by Jesus' defense of the woman. Isn't Jesus
the one who has taught us to feed the hungry, to give
drink to the thirsty, to clothe the naked, and to do many
other things that require money? Yet here he is, allowing
the woman to waste a year's wages on his feet! How are
we, who measure the worth of everything by what it
costs, to understand Jesus, who is not at all impressed
with our reliance on monetary values?

It is Jesus who provides the context for the woman's
disturbing recklessness. More keenly than anyone else at
the dinner, he knows what the week holds for him.

Death is much on his mind. He doesn't see Mary's gift as wastefulness, but as the responsible act of one who loves a dying friend. "It was intended that she should save this perfume for the day of my burial." It is another way of saying, "I'm already a dead man. She's preparing my corpse for burial." The expensive perfumed nard is thus not being squandered; it's being put to its intended purpose.

Judas, then, is like the greedy relative hovering over his rich uncle's deathbed, begrudging the money spent to keep him in the hospital, to pay the doctors, to prolong his life. In his heart of hearts he wants his uncle dead, lest his stubborn clinging to life should reduce the size of the estate. Yet the uncle had labored to accumulate the money so that he wouldn't be a burden on the family in his old age; his estate's first responsibility is to do what it is doing. Only what's left belongs to the nephew.

In this episode, nothing belongs to Judas but his greed.

Mary, on the other hand, whether she fully discerned all that Jesus did or not, is in her way entering into his sacrifice. He is giving his life; she is giving her means. He must in time bear his cross alone, but his pain will be assuaged by the knowledge that at least one cares, and she cares extravagantly.

Then Jesus surprises us again. He utters what seems a hard saying, out of character for this lover of the poor. "You will always have the poor among you, but you will not always have me." Is he turning his back on the impoverished? Is his grief so great, his own suffering so intense, that it has blotted out of his consciousness and his conscience the omnipresent demands of the needy?

To the contrary, the universality of their needs and the incessant nature of their demands trigger his comment. Always and always you can take care of those who can't care for themselves. You could and you should have been doing for them all along. But there is an opportunity for you today that you'll not have again. Tomorrow this woman can do nothing for me; today she can. She is seizing her opportunity. You are not. Don't use a new-found concern for the poor as a cover for your cupidity.

Here we must pause a few moments. What has seemed at first reading to be a clash of Mary's and Judas's values, with Jesus the judge declaring for Mary, now appears to hold an even more momentous lesson. Mary is not wrong in ministering to Jesus. Nor, although his motives are suspect, does Judas sin in speaking on behalf of the poor. The burden of Jesus' retort to Judas has rather to do with Judas's failure to seize the opportunity to do good appropriate to the occasion, to offer praise while he can, to celebrate life in the face of death.

As one who has watched a multitude of lost possibilities pass him by, I was also late in hearing what Jesus teaches here. Often hesitant, cautious by nature, timid when boldness is called for, I have robbed myself of many of the opportunities God has placed in my way. The older man I'm becoming is sometimes resentful of the younger man I once was because I wasn't bold enough to seize those openings. Sometimes in a darker mood I ponder what might have been. Fortunately, God has not been stingy with opportunities. I did take hold of others and found him in them, eager to bless.

It often seems to me that the difference between finding success in life and not finding it is less in personality or education or "luck," and more in an individual's taking advantage of opportunities that others shun. Let me give you a homely illustration of this principle. In 1902 Meyer Kubelski, a Jewish immigrant from Russia, gave his son Benjamin a fifty-dollar violin for his eighth birthday. That was back when fifty dollars was worth fifty dollars, a considerable sum to spend on a small boy. But the son loved music and was soon skilled enough to offer concerts at the Barrison Theater in Waukegan, his hometown. At eighteen he entered Vaudeville, having teamed up with a woman pianist.

In one concert, Benjamin Kubelski felt the urge between numbers to share with his audience a funny incident that happened to him. They laughed—and he loved it. Humor became a staple in his program. More than that, it took over his performance. Kubelski changed his name to Jack Benny and became one of the most successful and beloved comedians in this century. No one doubts that his comedic skills took him further than his musical skills would have done. He seized his opportunity.

Albert Einstein was a famous exploiter of opportunities. Often portrayed as the quintessential absent-minded professor, Einstein was really so present to the problem his mind was attacking that he was absent from more mundane considerations. Lord Samuel once wrote of him, "I have seen him in his keenness, when no table was handy, kneel down on the floor and scribble diagrams and equations on a scrap of paper on a chair."[4]

As a writer, I have taken heed to author Flannery O'Connor's way of waiting for the opportunity:

Many times, I just sit for three hours with no ideas coming to me. But I know one thing: If an idea does come between nine and twelve, I am there ready for it.[5]

As she implies, opportunities come more frequently to those who are prepared to seize them.

They sometimes don't look like breaks, though. Sometimes they look, as they do on this occasion for Jesus, like impending doom or failure. One of life's hardest lessons is this one: never quit just because you appear to be defeated. You may just be going through the difficult but necessary passageway to ultimate victory.

Gail Sheehy, in her study of successful persons, asked businessmen whether they had experienced any major failure in their professional or personal lives. She was surprised to learn that there was no difference between what the men who were most satisfied with their status in life and those who felt defeated had experienced. The most satisfied men were just as likely as the least to have had a flop. She then asked whether they considered it had been "a useful experience or a destructive one."

The high-satisfaction men said, "No one's immune. But there is one big difference. For me (and all but two of the men in my group) the failure was useful. I learned from it."

The low-satisfaction men confessed, "My failure destroyed something in me."[6]

The same experience of failure had been endured by both groups. One group learned and went forward to success. The other allowed the failure to defeat them. The difference is not in what happens to us but in who we are when it happens.

Jesus says in other Gospels that Mary's bold, imaginative grasping of the opportunity to do something for him would never be forgotten. It hasn't been.

Neither has Judas's dull failure to do so. Money blinded him. When you're mostly interested in money, you'll go for the quickest or highest return on your investment. Money values will color everything else.

When, like Mary's, your interest is in persons and relationships and the things of Christ, you'll not hesitate to sacrifice your money (or what you have bought with your money) to purchase a moment of blessing for the one you love. You will, to quote that old cliché, give up what you can't keep anyway to gain what you'll never lose.

Blessed are those who seize that opportunity. They're the life of the party.

---

[1]3 John 9, 10

[2]Victor Borge, *My Favorite Intermissions*. New York: Dorset, 1971, p. 54.

[3]*Time,* May 6, 1991, p. 26.

[4]Ronald W. Clark, *Einstein, the Life and Times*. New York: World Publishing, 1971, p. 175.

[5]Judith Appelbaum, *How to Get Happily Published*. New York: Harper and Row, 1988, p. 15.

[6]Gail Sheehy, *Pathfinders*. NY: Bantam Books, 1970, p. 102.

Chapter 8

When You Can't Keep People Quiet

Matthew 21:1-11; Luke 19:39-40

Jesus' triumphal entry is remembered every Palm Sunday all over Christendom. In our church it's one of our favorite seasons. With the processional of children waving branches as they enter the sanctuary while the choir belts out hallelujahs, the whole atmosphere is charged with enthusiasm.

"Hosanna to the Son of David!"

"Blessed is he who comes in the name of the Lord."

When Jesus entered Jerusalem, the entire city was stirred. The Palm Sunday spectacle is still an exhilarating one.

What means all this carrying on? How can we explain the mass fervor of so long ago, and the unabashed cheerfulness of a Palm Sunday crowd today?

Like many mass celebrations, this one isn't simple to interpret. It is, as Matthew is at pains to point out, a public announcement that, at long last, the Messiah has arrived in the holy city. Here he is, the Son of David, the Anointed One, the long-anticipated Savior!

It is more than that, also. Jesus does not ride a white horse trailing hostages behind him. He has no trophies of war. He rides humbly in an anti-triumph, the very opposite of the conquering generals who returned to Rome heading great parades to boast of their military victories. Jesus is Prince of Peace, not Commander-in-Chief of War.

The use of the donkey seems to be a calculated statement on Jesus' part about the nature of his kingdom.

But the rest is spontaneous, an act of the people, and it is rife with religious significance. As Luke points out, the people's spiritual leaders don't miss the meaning, and they don't like it. "Teacher, rebuke your disciples!"

Jesus is fully aware of what's going on. He will not do what the Pharisees ask because he cannot. You can't keep them quiet, he tells them. If you shut them up, the stones would cry out. You can't keep people from celebrating when they know they are in the approving presence of the Lord.

What is happening, then, is both spontaneous and elemental; it has not been orchestrated but has surged up from deep within the celebrants.

Praise Is Elemental

"Festivity, with its essential ingredients—excess, celebration, and juxtaposition—is itself an essential ingredient in human life,"[1] writes Harvey Cox. I read his *Feast of Fools* many years ago and have never been able to forget his argument. In those days, I was in a sense living a double life. On the one hand, the blessed life I enjoyed and my own sometimes irrepressible (my friends might have used the word *irresponsible* here) personality engendered a certain exuberance of behavior. I was, you might say, a noisy little man. Laughter punctuated the social gatherings I took part in. At the same time, though, my serious religious convictions seemed at odds with my happy noisiness. Serious Christians, it is assumed, are sober Christians. Not that my chief mentors had ever tried to teach me this near heresy, but plenty of other well-meaning disciples had. They are the religious descendants of that infamous medieval theologian, Petrus Cantor, who was known to have asked most ardently in the course of his ruminations whether Christ ever laughed. In fairness, I need to point out that Cantor was of the solemn opinion that Jesus must have if he was truly man, but that Cantor even felt the need to raise the question tells you quite a bit about

Cantor's, and medieval Christianity's, definition of spirituality.

As I said, Cox's book came to me at a propitious time. His defense of festivity helped me to appreciate what my limited grasp of the Christian faith had already led me to believe: not only is the "king who comes in the name of the Lord" to be blessed, but blessed indeed are those who are blessing him. They are justified in their merriment.

Cox convinced me (of course, I was an easy sell) that the loss of what he calls festivity "severs man's roots in the past and clips back his reach toward the future. It dulls his psychic and spiritual sensibilities."

Just a few years before *Feast of Fools* was published, our American religious sensibilities were shaken by the rise of the short-lived but challenging "Death of God" theology. Although it never appealed to me and provided conservatives with no end of hilarity at the expense of the humorless scholars, the godless school required an answer. Cox's was one of them. He shrewdly tied the heretical theology to the decline of festivity in Western industrial society and to the philosopher Nietzsche, who, while deploring the disappearance of festivity in Christendom, was the same man who gave us the phrase these theologians grasped. "God is dead," Nietzsche announced, and they echoed his cry nearly a century later. The effect, Cox argued, is predictable: you kill God, you kill celebration.

But for the exuberant celebrants on that first Palm Sunday, God was very much alive and at work in their midst. The gentle young man on the donkey's back was proof positive that God was not dead but was living and active and coming to their rescue. That's cause enough for a festival!

Praise is elemental. You can believe there is a God and withhold your worship, but you cannot believe *in* God, at least the God who sent Jesus, and keep from rejoicing.

God will be praised.

And God's people will praise him.

One of the most exciting things about our faith in God is the relief it brings. "Hosanna," the people cried. "Save us," is the original meaning of the word, which in time came to be an exclamation of praise. When you can praise the Savior and don't have to *be* a savior, your heart is lifted and your spirit rejoices.

Norman Vincent Peale tells of visiting a weary city leader who bewailed the heavy burden of responsibility he carried, having "the future destiny of people in my hands," an onus he hated. Dr. Peale eased the load a little by reminding him he didn't have their destiny in his hands at all; at worst he merely made some decisions that would affect their future, but he didn't determine their fate.

I would probably have been a little blunter. "You aren't their savior," I might have said. It's a lesson I had to learn myself; without it I couldn't have survived in the ministry. Having learned it, I join the throng in shouting "Hosanna" to the one who can save us.

Praise Is a Mark of Intelligence

You may want to accuse me of pushing this second point. If praise is basic to our very nature, both the smart and the not-so-smart will worship without even thinking about it. Intelligence has nothing to do with praise, you could argue. But I could offer this rebuttal: it is also a mark of intelligence to give expression to one's natural, elemental self rather than to fight against it.

John Updike helped me to understand this lesson. Not a theologian but a contemporary novelist who can't leave theological questions alone, Updike claims that ancient religion and modern science agree on the purpose of human existence: human beings are here to give praise or, as he perhaps more accurately puts it, "to pay attention," to look closely, without bias, at the marvelous world we inhabit. Updike calls attention to our "intellectual curiosity about the universe from the quasars down to the quarks, our delight and wonder at existence itself, and an occasional surge of sheer blind gratitude for being here."[2]

The more alert we are to the magnificence of our environment, the keener we are to discern its nearly incredible variety and charm, the stronger will be our impulse to praise. Is it any wonder that "How Great Thou Art" has remained one of our favorite hymns?

O Lord my God! When I in awesome wonder
Consider all the worlds Thy hands have made,
I see the stars, I hear the rolling thunder,
Thy power throughout the universe displayed,
Then sings my soul, my Savior God, to Thee:
How great Thou art! How great Thou art!
Then sings my soul, my Savior God, to Thee:
How great Thou art! How great Thou art!*

Don't let me mislead you, though. I am not assuming that so-called intellectuals will join the festivities. The Pharisees, learned Bible scholars that they are, will have nothing to do with rabble-rousing. Not for them the indecorous behavior of the uninformed. They call to mind Anatole France's sage remark, "I prefer the folly of enthusiasm to the indifference of wisdom." Dr. Peale, who writes so well on the subject of enthusiasm, adds: "Or shall we call it tired-out cynicism?"[3] Like France, he prefers enthusiasm because, as a doctor friend told him, people die from lack of it. "Of course, I can't write that on the death certificate, but the person without enthusiasm can lose the will to live."[4]

So the intellectual's sneer is not smart, not if it robs one of energy, hinders one from commitment, stifles spontaneity and excess, or leads to passive indifference.

Happiness is a choice, of course. In that very large crowd, not everyone is cheering. The Pharisees choose to frown.

Praise befits the intelligent because the intelligent choose to praise. They learn to like what uplifts them; in the words of a popular song of my childhood, they "accentuate the positive." They are like the schoolboy Francis Gay tells about who was learning to play the bassoon, no easy task for a youngster. This one was making such apparent progress he was asked to join an amateur orchestra. Mr. Gay asked how he was getting along.

"Well, Mr. Gay," said Jon, "we've got this new piece of music. It's very hard and I don't know whether I like it. But," he added, his face brightening, "I think I'll get to like it."[5]

An intelligent lad.

Praise Embraces the Absurd

One evening when Joy and I returned home from a Sunday school party, I was feeling somewhat remorseful and apologized to her for the fool I had made of myself. As is often typical of me when I'm with good friends, I was once again a noisy little man, singing a little too lustily, playing the piano too loudly, and in general making myself rather obnoxious. She calmed my fears. She said she worried about me only when I became too subdued at a party. It showed I was preoccupied, even worried. So long as I was being absurd, she knew I was all right.

If there's one point on which I think we Christians are underdeveloped, it's in our sense of the absurd. We take our faith—and ourselves—so seriously we fail to see just how ridiculous some things (including ourselves) really are. We praise God for the order in the universe, for how neatly he works things out. Sometimes, though, the workings of the Lord aren't all that tidy. He seems to delight in the unpredictable. Jesus' ride into Jerusalem is a case in point.

120

Because I grew up in Sunday school and have heard the story of Jesus' riding into Jerusalem on the back of a donkey all my life, it only recently dawned on me that there is a large element of the absurd in the story. Not until I went to college did I learn of the Roman triumphs, when the conquering generals rode into the capital astride a magnificent steed trailing their war booty (in goods and captured people) behind them. It was their finest moment; all eyes were on them, and they basked in the glory of their victory.

On Palm Sunday, however, Jesus rode on the back of a humble donkey. He brought no prisoners, displayed no spoils of war. He was more like an anti-hero. God must have been chuckling somewhere up in the highest. Chuckling, but not sneering. The spontaneous outpouring of people's exuberance, their salutes of palm branches and shouts of praise, were far, far better than the sullen silence of captured soldiers and the strutting self-importance of a general's retainers.

There is something childlike about praise. It doesn't stand on ceremony and isn't too much worried about propriety. That devout eighteenth-century literary giant Dr. Samuel Johnson, for example, startled his friends one morning after breakfast as they walked up a steep hill behind the house. When they reached the summit, he announced his intention to roll down the hill. They tried to talk him out of such foolishness, but he wouldn't be dissuaded. He said he hadn't had a good roll in a long time. He emptied his pockets, laid himself parallel with the edge of the hill, and rolled over and over until he reached the bottom. Rather an absurd thing for a grown man to do, his colleagues agreed, but sheer delight to Johnson, who relished life and loved all of God's creation.

Thinking of Dr. Johnson reminds me of something his old college companion, Oliver Edwards, once said. He admitted that he had tried in his time to be a philosopher but had failed because cheerfulness was always breaking in. I guess I'd have to confess I've tried to be a strait-laced disciple but have failed for the same reason.

It's all a matter of perspective, actually. Praise can see the ordinary through a laugh-producing prism. Florence Littauer's father brought cheerfulness into his home because, even when money was scarce, imagination wasn't. The family lived in three rooms behind their store. Laughter rang through those rooms, especially at mealtime, with her father commenting on politics and current events and stimulating his children's active minds with his provocative questions.

She remembers the day during World War II when he asked whether it would be possible "to make buildings that would go up and down to save on elevators?"

> Immediately we started on plans and verbally designed a skyscraper on pulleys. We began with the economy and ease of eliminating elevators and having the building move so businessmen could get out on their own floors. We put light switches on the outside of each door so that when the building sank, it would automatically light up each floor. Our design was also a great boon to window washers as they could do a whole skyscraper without ever getting off the ground.

A particularly appealing feature was the building's ability to sink rapidly into the ground during air raids. They designed the roof "as a pasture with peacefully grazing cows so that when the bombers flew over they would have no idea that under the cows was a business building."[6]

Absurd stuff, admittedly, but delightful, the play of intelligent minds looking at reality from a different perspective and celebrating the difference. It's kind of like sending a donkey into the city in place of a great white steed, and humble adults and children singing and shouting and praising God instead of watching a swaggering general dragging his captives behind.

Just absurd enough to be praiseworthy.

Violet Carter, reminiscing with an aging Winston Churchill, caught the old warrior in a peaceful mood. His mind wasn't on the fortunes of the British Empire or the glories of England's courageous stand against the Nazis. He was scouting butterflies and bemoaning their scarcity that summer. He told her that he sometimes thought of devoting part of his eightieth birthday fund to the creation of butterflies. He would appeal to people not to capture and destroy them but let them live and multiply.[7]

Not exactly what you would have expected the wartime leader to think so important. Almost absurd.

On this subject no one is more helpful than G. K. Chesterton, who made a career of turning everything around and around until he could study things from an angle generally overlooked by others. There was enough absurdity in his proclamations to force a smile from his sternest opponents. Oliver Herford captures the results in these verses:

> When plain folks such as you and I
> See the sun sinking in the sky,
> We think it is the setting sun:
> But Mr. Gilbert Chesterton
> Is not so easily misled;
> He calmly stands upon his head,
> And upside down obtains a new
> And Chestertonian point of view.
> Observing thus how from his toes
> The sun creeps closer to his nose
> He cries in wonder and delight
> How fine the sunrise is tonight![8]

As far as Chesterton is concerned, nothing is precisely what it seems. It's quite absurd, for example, to consider the young man on the humble donkey a threat to the Roman Empire, or to realize that he is the one who single-handedly defied Satan himself in the desert showdown, the Son of God and Son of Man, the terror of the

Temple whose fierce anger and bold action cleansed it of its money changers and other religious hucksters. He hardly looks the part. But look again. You see God's hand in it.

Praise Bursts Into Laughter

In our visit to Copenhagen we stood for a while before the statue of Denmark's famed theologian, Soren Kierkegaard. "The melancholy Dane," he is often called. Yet even he had an appreciation of the role of humor in religious faith. Doris Donnelly quotes him in an article on religion and humor. Kierkegaard had written of a dream he had when he was young:

> Something marvelous happened to me. I was caught up into the seventh heaven. There sat all the gods in assembly. As a special grace, there was accorded to me the privilege of making a wish. "Wilt thou," said Mercury, "wilt thou have youth, or beauty, or power, or long life, or the most beautiful maiden, or any other glorious thing among the many we have here in the treasure chest? Then choose but one thing." For an instant I was irresolute, then I addressed the gods as follows: "Highly esteemed contemporaries, I choose one thing, that I may always have the laugh on my side." There was not a god that answered a word, but they all burst out laughing. Thereupon, I concluded that my wish was granted, and I found that the gods knew how to express themselves with good taste.[9]

What does it mean to have "the laugh on my side"? Laughter is the mark of the winner, isn't it? It signifies security, assurance of victory; it bespeaks confidence. It belongs to the person who knows that, in spite of short-term difficulties, in the end all will be well.

We're back to perspective again. In drama, we name *tragedies* those plays that end in the fall of the hero. A *comedy* ends happily. When Dante wrote his greatest work he named it *The Divine Comedy*. It begins in Hell and continues through Purgatory, but it ends happily in Heaven.

Laughter is an appropriate expression of the praise of those who know that God will bring everything to a good conclusion.

Rome may mock the young man on his absurd little donkey, but the laugh is on Jesus' side.

The Pharisees may grumble that the crowds must be shut up, but the laugh is on Jesus' side.

The world may appear doomed and its inhabitants damned, but the laugh is on the side of Jesus' disciples.

Jack McDaniel's tale of his toil with the water tank could be read as a tragedy or comedy. It all depends on where you place the end of the story. Not a professional builder, missionary McDaniel says the most durable earthly structure he ever built was a water tank. He took on the task of constructing it because the family's only source of water was a spring that flowed from a steep hillside. He devoted his two-week vacation to hauling cement and sand and fabricating the four-inch-thick concrete walls, which he interlaced with half-inch steel. A solid piece of work. He built it to last for several lifetimes.

It didn't. Almost as soon as McDaniel was finished the water tank's service was over. Early one morning the soaked soil of the hillside, after suffering a deluge of rain, gave way and slid to the bottom of a small valley. His masterpiece was buried under several feet of mud, still intact (McDaniel had done his job well) but useless.

It isn't hard to imagine the missionary's dismay when he surveyed the damage. He tells the tale with a smile now, though. He says his experience with his tank has helped him enjoy the work he does as a minister. "Neither moth, nor rust, nor mud slide can take it away."[11] This is far from a tragic tale; McDaniel, comparing the value of the tank with the worth of the souls among whom he ministers, can laugh at his misfortune. He has achieved a comic perspective on the whole affair. The laugh is on his side.

One last thought. Children aren't specifically mentioned in any of the Gospel accounts of Jesus' triumphal entry, but I've never seen a Palm Sunday parade without them. In our church, we have an annual parade of children waving branches, carefully overseen by their teachers. It's a ritual we adults look forward to every year.

The Bible simply speaks of the crowd of disciples. If the Jerusalem of Jesus' day was anything like Jerusalem today, the children were there.

I thought about them when reading Bill Moyers' interview of Oren Lyons, chief of the Onodaga Indians. The chief was explaining the Indian method of passing the tribal heritage on to succeeding generations. "Our children are not sat down and taught about what's good and what's wrong. They see their grandfathers or they see their fathers or their grandmothers going to ceremonies. And they say, 'So that must be the right thing to do. The old people do it. Everybody does it. That's good.'"

So the tribal treasures are passed on, not by means of formal, classroom instruction but through group participation in honored ceremonies.

That's what it is, our Palm Sunday ritual. The children seem to be merely waving branches. But they are doing more, much more. They are paying homage to the man on the donkey. They are young and do not understand everything, but they do comprehend that the man is special. Their parents and their grandparents are remembering an important event when the young man chose to ride into Jerusalem on a humble donkey rather than a great white horse. He was turning things upside down, bringing the comic perspective to bear on a somber event, and the people were laughing and shouting. "So," as Lyons would say, "respect is learned through ceremony as a process."[11]

The church has wisely used ceremony to teach the greatest truths of the faith. What are baptism and Communion, Christmas and Easter pageants, and other dramatic and musical presentations if not ceremonious means by which to pass on to the next generation truths that must not be forgotten? The children watch and learn.

When they watch the triumphal entry being reenacted, they learn praise. They learn that Jesus is the reason to celebrate.

[1]Harvey Cox, *Feast of Fools: A Theological Essay on Festivity and Fantasy.* Cambridge: Harvard, 1969, p. 26.

[2]in *The Meaning of Life.* David Friend and the editors of *Life.* New York: Little, Brown.

[3]Norman Vincent Peale, *Enthusiasm Makes the Difference.* Greenwich, Conn.: Fawcett Publications, 1967, p. 14.

[4]Peale, *Enthusiasm,* p. 51.

[5]Francis Gay, *The Friendship Book.* London: D.C. Thomson and Company, Ltd., 1991, January 15.

[6]Florence Littauer, *The Pursuit of Happiness.* Eugene, Oregon: Harvest House, 1978, pp. 11, 12.

[7]Violet Carter, *Winston Churchill.* New York: Harcourt, Brace and World, Inc., 1965, p. 121.

[8]Maisie Ward, *Gilbert Keith Chesterton.* New York: Sheed and Ward, 1943, p. 586.

[9]From *Theology Today.* Quoted by Martin Marty, *Context,* June 15, 1992, p. 6.

[10]Jack McDaniel, "Things of Permanent Value," *Christian Standard,* October 27, 1991, p. 13.

[11]Bill Moyers, *A World of Ideas.* New York: Doubleday, 1990, p. 183.

Chapter 9

Celebration and Beyond

John 21:1-17

Have you ever done anything so offensive—to yourself, to someone who loves you, to God himself—that you couldn't stand to be in your own company? That your tears were bitter, stinging, nearly interminable?

When did you get over your crying?

Did you wonder whether you could look somebody in the eye again, ever, particularly if you'd already looked and seen and then couldn't wipe away the image of those eyes burning in yours?

When Jesus—betrayed, denied, tried on phony charges, condemned to die—caught Peter's eye in the courtyard, his unblinking gaze pierced Peter's bravado. His self-respect lay limp in the pitiless dirt. He would never forget that look.

How did he survive? Can you imagine his tormented mind, his pained heart, Friday, Saturday, into Sunday, wishing he could undo what he had done, could have been what he wasn't, could have said what he didn't? He needed a fresh start, a chance somehow to make things up to his friend, a new beginning.

A new beginning is the subject of John 21:1-17, although it doesn't seem so unless, while you read it, you are remembering what Peter did to Jesus in the courtyard that awful Thursday evening. Then what Jesus does here makes sense. The impromptu beach party takes place sometime after Jesus' resurrection. He has already put in a few appearances among his disciples, but one bit of unfinished business remains. He takes care of it here, at an early morning fish fry.

The disciples have been out on the lake all night. Even professional fishermen like these men occasionally come in empty handed. All night and no fish. On the shore they spot a figure who appears to know them.

"Friends," he calls to them, "haven't you any fish?"

"No," they answer.

And he says, "Throw your net on the right side of the boat and you'll find some."

Strange words. Only a few feet separate the right from the left side of a small Galilean fishing boat. What difference can it possibly make on which side they let the net down? They don't debate with the man, however. Do they already suspect who he might be? Doing as he has instructed, they hit a school of fish so large their net cannot contain the catch. Their success has opened their eyes to the stranger.

> Then the disciple whom Jesus loved said to Peter, "It is the Lord!" As soon as Simon Peter heard him say, "It is the Lord," he wrapped his outer garment around him (for he had taken it off) and jumped into the water. The other disciples followed in the boat.

> When they got to the shore, Jesus said to them:

> "Bring some of the fish you have just caught."
> Simon Peter climbed aboard and dragged the net ashore. It was full of large fish, 153, but even with so many the net was not torn. Jesus said to them, "Come and have breakfast." None of the disciples dared ask him, "Who are you?" They knew it was the Lord. Jesus came, took the bread and gave it to them, and did the same with the fish. This was now the third time Jesus appeared to his disciples after he was raised from the dead (John 21:7, 8, 10-14).

What can we make of this surprising reunion?

Celebrating What You Have

First came the catch, then breakfast from the catch. I'm stretching the point, to be sure, yet not much. It's an important life principle: you must take your celebrations where you find them, using what you have. It's your state of mind that makes the difference, not the circumstance.

What, then, is required for a party? Here, only several freshly caught fish, some burning coals, a little bread, and a few good friends. The secret is not in the glitter of the instruments but in the generosity of the host and guests. The most successful parties I have ever attended did not achieve their status by the opulence of the host's provisions but by the shared laughter, love, and hearts of the participants.

So celebrate with what you have.

Romuald Spasowski, running for his life, found a celebratory moment in the most dire circumstances. A student in Warsaw when Hitler's Nazis overran Poland, his life had been forever upended. The student had become the refugee, without a home, without bread, without security. Desperate, he abandoned his sanctuary in the Soviet-run refugee shelters in Lutsk and made his solitary way to the outskirts of the city. Not knowing the area, he wandered into a poor neighborhood crammed with people huddling in one-story, dilapidated hovels along both sides of the road. He stopped in front of one such shanty and begged, identifying himself as a student refugee from Warsaw. All he wanted was a place to stay. "It doesn't have to be much of anything."

The short Polish woman answered in Yiddish. "Please come in." Inside, he told her his story, sipping the tea she offered him as her two little children peered curiously from the other room. She had no room, she explained, but thought she could maybe put the children on straw mattresses, freeing a bed. When her husband came home they'd talk it over.

Never before had he so longed for a warm drink and a place to rest. Never had he felt so tired. The few simple potato pancakes she offered seemed like rare delicacies.

When her husband arrived, she and he conferred for what seemed like hours. Obviously he did not share her eagerness to help the poor student. But in the end, he relented. "Well, you stay here with us—but God only knows how we'll manage."

"I'll help you as much as I can," Spasowski assured him, and thought to himself, *How little a person needs if he has nothing at all.*[1]

It was very little, but it was enough, and Spasowski was thankful. He celebrated what he had.

Reading this section of Spasowski's story, I thought of Jesus' puzzling words in the Sermon on the Mount, as recorded by Luke:

> Blessed are you who are poor,
>   for yours is the kingdom of God.
> Blessed are you who hunger now,
>   for you will be satisfied (Luke 6:20, 21).

Only after a lifetime of ministry am I beginning to understand these abbreviated verses. Matthew's recall of Jesus' teaching is easier to grasp: "Blessed are the poor *in spirit,*" and "Blessed are those who hunger and thirst *for righteousness.*" Matthew moves the emphasis from physical poverty and hunger to spiritual humility and eagerness to have a right relationship with God and other persons. Somehow that is easier for to grasp. Luke does not spiritualize, however. He quotes Jesus as flatly preferring actual poverty and hunger. What could he possibly mean?

The answer is in the "woes" Luke appends to his version of the Beatitudes.

> Woe to you who are rich,
>   for you have already received your comfort.

Woe to you who are well fed now,
   for you will go hungry (Luke 6:24, 25).

The comfort of the rich is their wealth. They hoard it, guard it, take their pleasure in it—but have difficulty sharing it. Their comfort is in their possessions and not in their relationship with persons. Having much, they feel no need to reach out; having much, they feel a great need to keep others from reaching them. There is no further comfort for them.

Being able to feed themselves now, they have no need to seek sustenance from another. They have little desire to share what they have, either. They have fed their bellies but starved their relationships. They are alone.

It has long been a matter of record that the poor are proportionately far more generous than the rich. Parties among the fabulously wealthy are displays of their largesse. Parties among the very poor are a simple sharing of the little they have—like some hot coals, a little bread, some freshly caught fish, and good friends.

Celebrating Where You Are

The poor can express their joy wherever they are. For Jesus and his disciples, the Galilean shoreline early one morning was the place for their spontaneous barbecue.

Reading the account, you can't miss the overtones of Communion, not in a fine cathedral or even a plain chapel, but where they were, in the sand by the water.

"Jesus came, took the bread and gave it to them, and did the same with the fish" (John 21:13).

Bread and fish, reminiscent of the loaves and fishes that fed the five thousand. Commonplace food. Hardly the stuff of a party. But when touched by Jesus, it is transformed.

The bread and wine of the Last Supper were also commonplace. But when he broke the bread and poured the wine, when he prayed and distributed these simple elements to his disciples, the ordinary became extraordinary.

133

We remember the place where that Last Supper took place. We honor the hillside where tradition says he fed the five thousand. We make pilgrimages to the shores of Galilee because Jesus labored—and partied—there.

Some folks miss out on life's joy because they can't celebrate until everything is just right. I know of a husband who worked sacrificially to build his wife a new house. The home they had was quite adequate, but she was not satisfied because this or that wasn't quite up to par. So he built her a new one, although the strain that it put on his finances later caused him to lose his business. He tried diligently to do everything right. He bought the best furnishings and appliances. Still she wasn't content, and the big new house that he had hoped would be the scene of many joyous occasions with their friends welcomed few visitors. She couldn't entertain until everything was just right.

Often, when things have been less than perfect, I have meditated on Paul's excellent advice:

"Rejoice in the Lord always; I will say it again: Rejoice!" This is the same man who urges us to give thanks "in everything." If you insist on the ideal, you'll forego the possible.

Romuald Spasowski celebrated in the safety and with the meager portions his impoverished hosts offered him. David Jacobsen, held hostage for years by his Lebanese captors, discovered the joy of celebrating Communion daily, sometimes twice a day, even in captivity. He and his fellow prisoners called themselves the Church of the Locked Door.

Now that we were living together, we conducted services as often as twice a day, alternating between Ben's Protestant offering and Marty's Catholic mass. We took turns saving a piece of the breakfast pita bread to use as the Eucharist. For the morning service it would be fresh and soft but by evening as it dried out the pita turned hard and brittle like a cracker. . . . Since no one was in a rush to get out of the parking lot before the traffic jam or hit the first tee before the crowd, these were leisurely services.[2]

They learned the lesson Jesus taught the woman at the well in Samaria, who wondered precisely where God is to be worshiped.

> Believe me, woman, a time is coming when you will worship the Father neither on this mountain nor in Jerusalem. . . . A time is coming and has now come when the true worshipers will worship the Father in spirit and truth, for they are the kind of worshipers the Father seeks. God is spirit, and his worshipers must worship in spirit and in truth (John 4:21, 23, 24).

The God whom Christians worship is not confined to temple or shrine or church. Neither, then, is the celebration of his presence or of one another in his presence to be relegated to some supposedly holy spot. You can celebrate where you are.

Celebrating the Presence

The immediate cause of the disciples' rejoicing was not the huge catch of fish. They were celebrating being with Jesus. "None dared ask, 'Who are you, Lord?'" John says (21:12), because they knew. They had seen him in two other post-resurrection appearances. When he came to them, they were not anticipating him but were tending their own affairs, as if Jesus were teaching them (and us) that, never far from them, he could materialize in their midst at any moment. They always dwelt in his presence. "Where two or three come together in my name, there am I with them," he had earlier promised them (Matthew 18:20). Now he was demonstrating what the promise means. He had dissolved the barrier between secular and sacred, between the spirit and material worlds.

Leslie D. Weatherhead finds many reasons for celebrating Jesus' closeness. When we are sensitive to his nearness, "men hate sin with a new hatred," including our own baseness. Paradoxically, however, we "are not driven into inferiority" as we surely would be could we come into proximity with any other great historical figure.

Jesus' presence delivers us out of our selfishness into "a new kingdom of creative values," in which through perfect self-forgetfulness we are "really able to express [ourselves] perfectly." This new freedom from self enables us to grasp what Augustine was getting at when he said, "Love God and do what you like."

"We are delivered from all the country of selfhood into the country of otherness. . . ." Weatherhead spells out the different effect Jesus has on us:

St. Paul would make men feel cowards. Grenfell and Schweitzer would make most of us feel babies. Wordsworth makes one feel coarse and dull. Lincoln makes one feel impatient and tactless. The real scholar makes one feel an ignoramus. The real saint makes one feel a sinner. But the presence of Jesus makes one feel utterly humbled and *yet utterly exalted.* He makes one feel one could do and be anything.[3]

Weatherhead has described the disciples' gladness to be with Jesus here. And our own. Is it any wonder that a certain old hymn just won't die? Scorned by theologians and high churchmen, no other song is more widely requested at funerals than "In the Garden." It's the chorus that expresses the believer's mystical union with Christ, his sense of humble exaltation in being in his presence:

And he walks with me
And he talks with me,
And he tells me I am his own.

Alone, yet not alone, the celebrant rejoices in the company of the Lord. The place is a matter of indifference.

Paul, writing in prison of all places, could still rejoice. So can we.

Celebrating the Completed Circle

When Jesus was buried, the company of disciples scattered. But now, for the moment, he is back with them. Their group feels whole again.

So it must seem to Peter, especially when Jesus singles him out for reconciliation. On that fateful night, Peter had denied his Lord ("I don't know the man"). Now Jesus is at pains to convince Peter he is back in Jesus' good graces. Three times Peter denied Jesus; three times Peter affirms him.

I'm thinking of a recent Christmas. We were all together for the first time in many years. Seventeen of us in our small house, stepping on things, sitting anywhere, stumbling over feet, laughing, crying, reminiscing, luxuriating in each other's presence. We were together; the circle was complete. Like most families, most of us nestle together in the center of our love, but we have one or two who feel they function better out on the edge, doing their thing, tethered to the family but straining against the rope from time to time. They, too, were home, and it was heaven.

Peter had been at tether-length, too. Nobody exiled him; he put himself there. He couldn't deny he had denied Jesus. And there was that look. Always he could see the look. He couldn't shake his ambivalence. He wanted to see Jesus—and was a little afraid. He knew they had to take care of that unfinished business. It wouldn't be easy.

Let me ask it again: have you ever done something really unforgivable and you knew it was up to you to effect the reconciliation? You knew you had to go and beg forgiveness, and you didn't want to? And while you were mentally forming your words, rehearsing your speech, suddenly you were listening and another was talking, and what you were hearing were words leading to the very reconciliation you wanted.

When they had finished eating, Jesus said to Simon Peter, "Simon, son of John, do you truly love me more than these?"

"Yes, Lord," he said, "you know that I love you."

Jesus said, "Feed my lambs."

Again Jesus said, "Simon son of John, do you truly love me?"

He answered, "Yes, Lord, you know that I love you."

Jesus said, "Take care of my sheep."

The third time he said to him, "Simon son of John, do you love me?"

Peter was hurt because Jesus asked him the third time, "Do you love me?" He said, "Lord, you know all things, you know that I love you" (John 21:15-17).

In Peter's answer are not only the response to the question, but his heart's cry for forgiveness and acceptance, "Lord, you know I love you." He didn't say it, but he was also telling Jesus, "I didn't mean what I did. I'm so sorry. In spite of what I did, I want you to know I love you."

Jesus knew, but Peter needed to learn one thing more. Three times Peter had denied him; three times Jesus took him through this exercise, as if to say each exchange canceled one denial. But more than words was required.

I had a little altercation with one of the grandsons on the Christmas day I was telling you about. We live in an A-frame house with a loft. My study is up there. That's holy ground, as least as far as inquisitive, destructive grandchildren are concerned. Besides, it's not an altogether safe place for little ones, since only a rather widely spaced banister railing separates them from the main floor. Hence the "no little grandchildren allowed here" rule. A rule guaranteed, as you can imagine, to bring out the spirit of adventure.

One little adventurer couldn't resist. He had to test Grandpa's resolve. As I was sitting on the stairs, he nestled beside me for a brief conversation. My part of it had to do with how he wasn't to go up into the loft. Then my attention was diverted to the entertainment on the main floor. In a trice he was gone. In less than a trice (a grandpa's rather slow-motioned trice, admittedly), I was in the loft. My grandson thus had his first opportunity to observe a side of my personality he had not met before.

"I'm sorry," he said, with all the glibness of one well practiced in displaying repentance.

"That's not good enough," I explained as I whisked him off his feet and replanted them on the first floor. "You are not to be on these steps again." And he wasn't.

Sometimes "I'm sorry" just doesn't work with Grandpas. Or with God. "Oh, God, I'm sorry. Now leave me alone." No, the Lord requires evidence of genuine repentance, as when Jesus tells Peter again and again, until he is convinced Peter has really heard him, that he must "feed my sheep, feed my sheep, feed my sheep."

Moving Beyond Celebration

Feeding sheep is moving beyond repentance to service, beyond celebration to usefulness in the kingdom, which is the greatest of all sources of joy.

When Peter wants to know about another disciple's fate, Jesus gently reminds him that Peter is asking something that is none of his business (John 21:21, 22). It is Peter's obedience, not John's, that the Lord is waiting for. To remain in Jesus' circle, you look after your own obedience; criticism of another's is forbidden.

So there they are. What began as a night of fishing ended as a celebration of the Lord and his now completed circle.

On this note John leaves his story. It's a good place to stop. Reconciliation has been effected, the community of Jesus' followers has been restored, and the memories of this party will linger as long as John's story will be read.

I once had the opportunity to hear Dr. Scott Peck address a large gathering of nurses in Phoenix. At the time he was writing a new book to be called *A Different Drummer.* When it was published I found the outline he had given us in one of his addresses. His thesis was that there are four stages in community building. It begins with what he calls pseudo-community, a stage in which the individuals strive self-consciously to act like a community but fail, because they are too self-centered.

Then comes chaos, with the members of the group falling away, unable to sustain a relationship with one another.

Then emptiness, the inner experience of those who had sought togetherness but floundered.

The final stage is community, in which sustained, mutually satisfying relationships are achieved.

Dr. Peck came to this outline through his investigation of how groups are born and flourish. He must have included the New Testament in his research, for his four stages perfectly outline the experience of Jesus' disciples. In the beginning, when Jesus was with them, he held them by the magnetism of his personality, the brilliance of his teaching, the marvel of his miracles, and the way he seemed to be realizing their own expectations. When he "failed" them in Jerusalem, their pseudo-community was shattered into chaos, their devotion replaced by emptiness and drifting. Only at the end, after he had appeared to them several times to deal with unfinished business (Peter's denial, Thomas' doubt, the disciples' general lack of direction and power) did they become a genuine group, a community of believers inspired by the same Spirit and directed by the same commission, committed to him and to one another.

From now on their circle would be unbroken, and forevermore Jesus' disciples would be identified not as individuals on a solitary quest, but as disciplined members of one another who shared each other's woes and echoed each other's laughter.

If Dr. Peck is correct in his study of community-building, we can easily see why so many individuals in our alienated society are lonely and sad. They may belong to clubs, social societies, sororities, fraternities, or other pseudo-communities, but they still feel no real sense of belonging. Real community cannot be attained by joining some*thing*; it is created when you join some*one*, or several someones, in a relationship marked by integrity, acceptance, and commitment to each other and to something or someone bigger than either of you.

Even laughter, that basic human response to the comic, requires another person for full enjoyment. Traveling by myself quite a bit, I have attended the theater alone on several occasions. My enjoyment is always diminished when there is no one for me to nudge, to look in the eye, to reinforce my mirth. As Henri Bergson has observed,

> Laughter appears to stand in need of an echo. Listen to it carefully: it is not an articulate, clear, well-defined sound; it is something which would fain be prolonged by reverberating from one to another. . . .[4]

You can cry alone, but you cannot really celebrate alone. You need the circle. And you need to move beyond celebration to mission and service.

Sometimes it is called feeding sheep.

[1]Romuald Spasowski, *The Liberation of One*. San Diego: Harcourt Brace Jovanovich, 1986, pp. 82-84, italics mine.

[2]David Jacobsen with Gerald Astor, *Hostage: My Nightmare in Beirut.* New York: Donald I. Fine, 1991, p. 108.

[3]Leslie D. Weatherhead, *Jesus and Ourselves*. London: Epworth, 1930, p. 259.

[4]Henri Bergson, *Laughter,* Quoted in *Great Treasury of Western Thought,* ed. Mortimer J. Adler and Charles Van Doren. New York and London: R. R. Bowker, 1977, p. 1052.

Chapter 10

The *Big* Event

Luke 24:50-53 Acts 1:6-11, Revelation 7:9-17

The believer's best party of all is yet to come.

It won't take place in your lifetime, not until you've run your race and finished your course, not until you've replaced your earthly tent for a more permanent dwelling, your corruptible body for an imperishable one. Not on this soil, not in this lifetime, not on this planet.

That's because God has saved the best for the last. In a very real sense, a Christian's faith always faces forward. He is not like the elder who stood beside the Communion table and prayed, "Lord, help us to think back to when your Son was still living." The Christian's Lord *is* still living, and is present in the present and already present in the future, to which he beckons his disciples. Wonderful things have happened in the past, and this book has recounted some of them, but they pale when compared with the splendor yet to come. The really BIG event lies ahead.

The disciples thought they had seen it all. Now, at last, after the years of vacillating, they had come to full belief in Jesus. They had thought they were believers before, but that was before the real test. When he was arrested, tried, convicted, and executed, they were shattered. Why hadn't he called his twelve legions of angels[1] to protect him? Why had he so meekly submitted to the manhandling? Why hadn't the one who could call Lazarus back from the grave kept himself out of one?

143

But that was then and this was now. He had come back. He had walked and talked and eaten among them and they knew, they knew for sure, that he was indeed the Son of the living God.

The resurrection was persuasive proof. It made all the difference.

French thinker Auguste Comte once told Thomas Carlyle that he was going to start a new religion to replace Christianity. "Very good," replied Carlyle.

> All you will have to do is to be crucified, rise again the third day, and get the world to believe you are still alive. Then your new religion will have a chance.[2]

Jesus' disciples believed. His new religion had a chance. But, as far as the disciples were concerned, everything was not yet tidied up. "Lord, are you at this time going to restore the kingdom to Israel?" (Acts 1:6).

They were your basic conservatives, these disciples. Like most of the rest of their countrymen, they had suffered under the yoke of Rome long enough. They wanted Jewish independence, and they believed Jesus could deliver it. They wanted restoration. They wanted to go back to when things were better.

Jesus wanted something far different, far better, something that lay in the future, not in the familiar past. Luke doesn't spell it out, either in his Gospel or in Acts. Instead, he records Jesus' words. "It is not for you to know the times or dates the Father has set by his own authority." In other words, I'm not going to answer your question. I'm going to do something far better: "But you will receive power when the Holy Spirit comes on you; and you will be my witnesses. . ." (Acts 1:7, 8). I am going to empower you and dispatch you. You have work to do.

But that still isn't the end of the matter. He had earlier promised them that, when he finally left them, it would be only for a while and only for a wonderful purpose: "I am going there to prepare a place for you." Where? To "my Father's house." What will he do then? "I will come back and take you to be with me" (John 14:1-4).

As they stand there, gazing into heaven after him, they have forgotten. Hence the angel, who reminds them: "This same Jesus, who has been taken from you into heaven, will come back in the same way you have seen him go into heaven" (Acts 1:11). Then they remembered. "Of course, he's coming back for us!"

Ascended into Heaven, he would descend from Heaven. The barrier between earth and Heaven would be rent, like the veil of the temple. Time and eternity would stand united, earth and Heaven joined, here and hereafter a continuum, and in God's eternal dwelling place, the ultimate celebration has already begun!

But what will it be like?

As I said, Luke leaves the question unanswered. His task as biographer and historian is to record the earthly life and ministry of Christ (Gospel of Luke) and the establishing of his new church (Acts). For the rest of the story, we have to turn to John's Apocalypse, the Book of Revelation. Here we learn that the *Big Event* is the victory celebration of the saints when their mission on earth is over.

In the meantime, of course, the saints must do the work he assigns: "You'll be my witnesses." Acts and the epistles record and comment on how they carried out their assignment. It is left to the book of Revelation to vouchsafe a preview of the eternal party, in which the victory has been won and the saints have been gathered in.

In the meanwhile, though, the battle rages, and believers remain on the field, being the Lord's witnesses, doing their Master's bidding. The time for complacency has not yet come. Joseph Tson, Romanian pastor now working in United States, said at Wheaton College that, although he had long predicted the collapse of communism, he nonetheless found some Christians reluctant to help him because of their conviction that the Bible predicts a Soviet victory. While Tson begged for assistance in trying to fill Russia's moral and intellectual and spiritual vacuums, one respondent said bluntly: "You can't do it. We are going to lose, communism is going to win, and in fact communism is going to so sweep the globe that Christians are going to be killed."

Gary DeMar of American Vision adds his own comments to Tson's lament:

> I am not just blasting people; instead I am saying there are implications to all this. For centuries, people have been predicting the end—and they have been wrong. Much of the mess we are in in our day is because Christians have sat back as eschatological couch potatoes and allowed the humanists to go ahead with their world view. Meanwhile, we haven't had anything to say to the world.[3]

Why has there been this confusion about our task, this refusal to enter the fray? Has Jesus changed his orders? How can one read the New Testament and not conclude that evangelism must continue, churches must be planted, nations must be liberated? Remember Jesus' reading of Isaiah 61 (in Luke 4) in the synagogue in his home town?

> The Spirit of the Lord is on me,
> because he has anointed me
> to preach good news to the poor.
> He has sent me to proclaim freedom
> for the prisoners
> and recovery of sight for the blind,
> to release the oppressed,
> to proclaim the year of the Lord's favor.

Jesus applied this Scripture to himself, pointing to its fulfillment in his own person. It is the business he came to accomplish, business that remains unfinished to this day.

146

Gregory L. Fisher, teaching in a West African Bible college, was asked by one of his students, "What will he say when he shouts?" Fisher, not understanding the question, asked for clarification.

"First Thessalonians 4:16 says that Christ will descend from Heaven with a loud command. I would like to know what that command will be."

Earlier that day Fisher had had an encounter with a refugee from the Liberian civil war.

> The man, a high school principal, told me how he was apprehended by a two-man death squad. After several hours of terror, as the men described how they would torture and kill him, he narrowly escaped. After hiding in the bush for two days, he was able to find his family and escape to a neighboring country. The escape cost him dearly: two of his children lost their lives. The stark cruelty unleashed on an unsuspecting, undeserving population had touched me deeply.
>
> I also saw flashbacks of the beggars that I pass each morning on my way to the office. Every day I see how poverty destroys dignity, robs men of the best of what it means to be human, and sometimes substitutes the worst of what it means to be an animal. I am haunted by the vacant eyes of people who have lost all hope."
>
> "Enough," I said. "He will shout, '*Enough!*' when he returns."

A look of surprise opened the face of the student. "What do you mean, enough?"

> "Enough suffering. Enough starvation. Enough terror. Enough death. Enough indignity. Enough lives trapped in hopelessness. Enough sickness and disease. Enough time. Enough!"[4]

Can't you imagine the Lord, his heart breaking, doing just that? Proud of his followers who fight the evil on

147

every front but seeing them overwhelmed by the odds, he announces they have done enough. It is over. They can enter into their rest.

It is that rest that John has glimpsed in his vision of heaven.

The Future Unveiled

There they are, "a great multitude that no one could count, from every nation, tribe, people and language" (Revelation 7:9), home at last. They have sojourned all over earth's surface where they have endured great tribulation in the ongoing battle. Their struggle for survival is over, their encounter with evil behind them. They are before the heavenly throne, and they are having a wonderful time.

Times weren't always good on earth. Jesus had warned his disciples. Their story would have a happy ending, but in the meantime:

> Do not suppose that I have come to bring peace to the earth. I did not come to bring peace, but a sword (Matthew 10:34).

> Watch out that no one deceives you. For many will come in my name, claiming, "I am the Christ," and will deceive many. You will hear of wars and rumors of wars, but see to it that you are not alarmed. Such things must happen, but the end is still to come. Nation will rise against nation, and kingdom against kingdom. There will be famines and earthquakes in various places. All these are the beginning of birth pains.
>
> Then you will be handed over to be persecuted and put to death, and you will be hated by all nations because of me. At that time many will turn away from the faith and will betray and hate each other, and many false prophets will appear and deceive many people. Because of the increase of wickedness, the love of most will grow cold, but he who stands firm to the end will be saved (Matthew 24:4-13).

Jesus never blinked when he gazed into the future. Neither did he withhold what he saw from his disciples. He made no promise of continuous happiness on earth.

On the other hand, while he does not withhold the bad news from his disciples, neither does he keep the good news secret. He is going away, he tells them in John 14:1-6, in order to prepare a place for his followers. When all is ready, he will come again and take us to himself.

John's Revelation tells in graphic but earthbound language something of what it'll be like, this place Jesus has gone to prepare. It will be a huge celebration, a mass of humanity "from every nation, tribe, people and language." It will feature the honored Host, whom they honor enthusiastically, having been so lavishly rewarded for their service to him.

The multitude of believers are at worship, carrying palm branches reminiscent of the day of Jesus' triumphal entry into Jerusalem. Then the cry arose, "Hosanna," which means "Lord, save us." Now they who have been saved are thanking God for their salvation.

Salvation belongs to our God,
who sits on the throne,
and to the Lamb (Revelation 7:10).

With gladness they "serve him day and night in his temple." One doesn't begrudge a little service to the one who has banished hunger, thirst, scorching heat, insecurity, and sorrow forever. "And God will wipe away every tear from their eyes" (Revelation 7:15-17).

If you have ever read Thomas Hardy's dark novel, *Tess of the d'Urbervilles,* you probably have had the same difficulty as I forgetting his bitter closing paragraph, after the life has gone out of the tragic Tess. Hardy speaks of "the dreaming, dark, dumb thing that turns the handle of the idle show." Then this chilling epitaph: "The President of the Immortals (in Aeschylean phrase) had ended his sport with Tess." When I first read the book, I was startled to find such an ugly sentence at the end of an otherwise stirring book by a usually careful author. Not only ugly in phrasing, but clumsy. Ugly also in its bitterness, the sentence is reminiscent of Shakespeare's heartbroken King Lear's lament:

As flies to wanton boys, are we to the gods;
They kill us for their sport.

No they don't, not according to Revelation, where there are no gods but God, and wherein the Lamb has been killed so the people can be saved. Grace and powerful justice, not wantonness and sport, are in charge. No wonder the people celebrate.

Like them we also celebrate, joining their song:

Crown him with many crowns, The Lamb upon the throne;
Hark! how the heavenly anthem drowns All music but its
   own;
Awake, my soul, and sing Of him who died for thee,
And hail him as thy matchless king Through all eternity.

Crown him the Lord of love; Behold his hands and side,
Rich wounds, yet visible above, In beauty glorified;
No angel in the sky Can fully bear that sight,
But downward bends his wond'ring eye At mysteries so
   bright.

Crown him the Lord of life, who triumphed o'er the grave,
And rose victorious in the strife for those he came to save;
His glories now we sing, who died and rose on high,
Who died, eternal life to bring, and lives that death may
   die.[5]

The Present Explained

My friend James C. Smith, longtime executive director of Christian Missionary Fellowship, devoted many months to the study of the missionary message in the book of Revelation. He writes of "the seven seals, seven trumpets, seven persons and seven bowls/plagues [that] are introduced by seven letters to seven churches, interspersed by sevenfold doxologies/hallelujahs, seven blessings/beatitudes, and finally climaxed by seven 'new things.'" All these are contained in the seven major points Jim finds in the book:

1. Almighty God has an eternal purpose and it is unfolding in history.
2. The Living Son is the One who opens the seals, i.e., the One who controls and gives meaning to this purpose.
3. Satan and his forces oppose that purpose and are committed to thwarting it.
4. This conflict grows in intensity, along with God's restrained judgments/wrath until a decisive and final battle.
5. God and his people win! Vengeance, vindication and victory are just, certain and eternal.
6. God climaxes all this with a new order of things including a new heaven and new earth.
7. The prayers of the saints (Revelation 5:8; 8:4, 5) participate in the unfolding of history. It is our one form of direct participation in the Reign of God. No wonder the Evil One seeks to divert us from this most important act. No wonder Jesus taught us to pray, "Thy kingdom come, thy will be done on earth as it is in heaven." The Book of Revelation describes how that prayer is being answered . . . for every tribe, people, tongue and nation.

And that is the focus of the Christian world mission.[6]

The mission to which Jesus assigns his disciples becomes personal. No one who accurately grasps the full import of the commission in Matthew 28 and Acts 1 can take life lightly again. Every believer has a mission to fulfill, a God to glorify, a life of incalculable importance to live now in anticipation of a great ingathering of redeemed souls later. We now understand concerning

151

ourselves specifically what Nels Ferre once learned about reality in general. He worked up enough courage to ask the great philosopher Alfred North Whitehead how he would characterize reality in one sentence. An impossible task, one would assume, but the bold thinker had a ready response: "It matters, and it has consequences." Further explanation was required. Whitehead said things matter to the maximum to us only when we are alive to the consequences of *our* lives, that depth of personal life cannot be achieved apart from depth of social concern.[7] Jesus calls his followers to exactly that depth of social concern, and they who follow him achieve a depth in their personal lives unattainable otherwise. They live consequentially. Their whole focus is now on others, not on themselves. They want their brief time on earth to make a difference in other people's lives. They are eager to carry out Christ's commission to the fullest.

Such persons don't think a great deal about heaven. They take Christ's promises for granted, but they are too busy making an impact on the here and now to spend much time dreaming about the Big Event to come. Neither do they worry much about themselves in the afterlife, what they will look like, how they will be known. In fact, their concern isn't for themselves at all. John Updike says it is not "ourselves in our nervous tics and optical flecks that we wish to perpetuate" in the afterlife but "ourselves as window on the world that we can't bear to think of shutting." He insists that "the yearning for life after death" is unselfish. "It is love and praise for the world that we are privileged, in this complex interval of light, to witness and experience"[8] that causes us to yearn forward. Yes, it is that, but it is more than that. It is the passion we have for other persons as well, a desire that they, too, should be saved, and that we shall know them forever.

The saints around the throne are not only enjoying the presence of God, they are enjoying each other. They are persons who learned long ago to seek their pleasure in loving the Lord and loving their neighbors. Now they get to do this forever.

Around the throne there are only the lovers and the loved, standing together, singing, praising, rejoicing, enjoying one another. There are no kings and peasants, no lords and lorded over. All are fellow servants before the only true Lord.

> It might suit a number of the lords
> if death fixed everything for ever
> confirmed eternally the lordship of the lords
> the servitude of the servants.
>
> It might suit a number of the lords
> to remain lords for ever
> in their costly private tombs
> their servants still serving
> in row on row of cheap graves.
>
> But there is a resurrection different from what we thought
> resurrection that is
> God's revolt against the lords
> and against the lord of lords: death.[9]

So in the Big Event, to be enjoyed forever by those whom the Lord calls to his party, there will be no lords but *the* Lord; all others will be his servants. And there will be death no more. For the Lord has banished death.

The Celebration Anticipated

How can we best describe the Big Event? How can we put the ineffable into descriptive language? Revelation does its best, but it only suggests. No one this side of heaven can do more than suggest, and every one uses his own earthly experience to picture the unearthly. Among the attempts, John Jasper's is one of my favorites. Born in slavery, given only enough schooling to read the Bible, this great preacher of the last century delivered the funeral sermon for a Mary Barnes, in which he paints a picture of the Big Event in terms far removed from Revelation's apocalyptic vision, but very close to his heart's hope. His message and the Bible's are the same. The faithful saint of the Lord can look forward to a homecoming that will compensate for everything suffered here.

My brethren, I often ask myself how I'd behave myself if I was to get to heaven. . . . [B]elieve I'll just down the town—walkin' and runnin' all roun' to see the home which Jesus done built for His people. First of all, I'd go down and see the river of life. . . . I longs for its crystal waves, and the trees on the banks, and the all manners of fruits. . . .

After that, I'd turn out and view the beauties of the city—the home of my Father. I'd stroll up them avenues where the children of God dwell and view their mansions. Father Abraham, I'm sure he got a great palace, and Moses. . . . and David, the king that made pretty songs, I'd like to see his home, and Paul the mighty scholar who got struck down out in the 'Mascus road, I want to see his mansion, and all of 'em.

Then I would cut roun' to the back streets and look for the little home where my Saviour's set my mother up to housekeepin' when she got there. I 'spect to know the house by the roses in the yard and the vine on the porch. Look there; mighty sweet house, ain't it lovely? Look there; see that on the door; hallelujah, it's John Jasper. Said He was gwine to prepare a place for me; there it is! Too good for a poor sinner like me, but He built it for me, a turn-key job, and mine forever. Oh, what must it be to be there!

And now, friends, if you'll 'scuse me, I'll take a trip to the throne and see the King in his royal garments. Oh, what it must be to be there!

My brethren, I done forgot somethin'. I got to take another trip. I ain't visited the ransom of the Lord. I can't slight them. I knows a heap of 'em, and I'm bound to see 'em. Here's Brer Abel, the first man whar' got here; here's

Brer Enoch whar' took a stroll and straggled into glory; here's old 'Ligie, whar' had a carriage sent for 'em and comed a higher way to the city. Here she is; I knowed she'd get here; why Mary Barnes, you got home, did you? Oh, what must it be to be there![10]

It's beyond imagining, that's what it's like to be there!

[1]See Matthew 26:53.

[2]Leighton Ford, "The Resurrection of Christ: A Matter of Public Record," *Focus on the Family*, March, 1986, p. 2.

[3]"The Bible As a Joke: New Book Warns Against Eschatological Game-Playing," *World*, October 26, 1991, p. 12.

[4]Gregory L. Fisher, "Second Coming," *Leadership*, Fall, 1991, p. 45.

[5]Words by Matthew Bridges (1851) and Godfrey Thring (1874).

[6]James C. Smith, "Generally Speaking," *Impact*, March-April, 1981, p. 2.

[7]Nels F. S. Ferre, *Making Religion Real*, p. 26. Italics mine.

[8]John Updike, *Self-Consciousness*. New York: Knopf, 1989, pp. 216, 217.

[9]Kurt Marti, *Leichenreden*. Neuwied and Berlin, 1969, p. 63. Quoted in Hans Kung, *Eternal Life?* Garden City, New York: Doubleday, 1984, p. 117.

[10]John Jasper, "A Picture of Heaven," in Clyde E. Fant, Jr. and William M. Pinson, Jr., eds, *Twenty Centuries of Great Preaching*, Vol. IV. Dallas: Word, Inc., 1971, pp. 328, 329. Used with permission.

Chapter 11

Getting Serious about Celebrating

Philippians 4:4-9

That earnest letter writer from Virginia (in the introduction) is still on my mind. Life is serious, he insists gravely, and certainly no substantial thinker in history would disagree with the fretful gentleman. Even humorist Garrison Keillor concedes, "Life is complicated and not for the timid. It's an experience that when it's done, it will take us a while to get over it."[1] Author Graham Greene, in an autobiography aptly entitled *Means of Escape,* finds life so very serious some means of flight from it is necessary.

> Writing is a form of therapy; sometimes I wonder how all those who do not write, compose or paint can manage to escape the madness, the melancholia, the panic fear which is inherent in the human situation.

Then he quotes with approval W. H. Auden, "Man needs escape as he needs food and deep sleep."[2]

Bertrand Russell chimes in from somewhere. "Life is nothing but a competition to be the criminal rather than the victim."[3] Not much to celebrate here, is there? Let me add one more. Plato partially agrees with the learned gentlemen, but hear him out, because he also agrees with the thesis of this book. "When you swear, swear seriously and solemnly, but at the same time with a smile, for a smile is the twin sister of seriousness."[4] Without both twins, life is lopsided.

The smile and the seriousness are welded in Paul's letter to his friends in Philippi, especially in 4:4-9. The counsel resonates with gladness and sobriety: *rejoice, rejoice, be gentle, do not be anxious, pray, petition, give thanks, present requests, think the highest thoughts, imitate me.*

Let's listen more closely.

"Rejoice in the Lord always. I will say it again: Rejoice!"

The mood is imperative. Do as I tell you. Take control of your emotions. Rejoice. Enjoy God. A strange order, this one, to a generation devoted to the pursuit of happiness apart from God rather than to joy in him. Stranger yet are the circumstances in which Paul writes. He is, as he says early in the letter, "in chains for Christ," a prisoner—a prisoner urging free persons to join in his gladness. He not only urges, but models the surprising behavior he demands. He leaves no room for excuses. How can you in your freedom complain to a captive?

Paul's assumption that joy is a quality over which we have control reminds one of Karl Barth's likening of the will for joy to the will for life. As far as Barth was concerned, our will to enjoy parallels our will to eat, drink, sleep, work, attain health, and be ethical and in fellowship with God. All other drives are subject to the will's supervision. So with the will to enjoy.

C. S. Lewis, who has written so wisely on the subject of joy ("the serious business of heaven"), makes it a topic for demonic analysis in his famous *Screwtape Letters*. It's fun to look at it through the eyes of Screwtape, the veteran fiend and value distorter *par excellence*. He speaks:

I divide the causes of human laughter into Joy, Fun, the Joke Proper, and Flippancy. You will see the first among friends and lovers reunited on the eve of a holiday. Among adults some pretext in the way of Jokes is usually provided, but the facility with which the smallest witticisms produce laughter at such a time shows that they are not the real cause. *What that real cause is we do not know.* Something like it is expressed in much of that detestable art which the humans call Music, and something like it occurs in Heaven—a meaningless acceleration in the rhythm of celestial experience, quite opaque to us. *Laughter of this kind does us no good and should always be discouraged.* Besides, the phenomenon is of itself disgusting and a direct insult to the realism, dignity, and austerity of Hell.[5]

Joy insults Satan. Screwtape doesn't understand it, can't fathom the source of it, so, like the ignorant and prejudiced everywhere, he advises his young protege Wormwood to discourage it among humans. It's not dignified. The laughter of joy is the antithesis of the "realism" of Hell, where there is nothing to laugh about and where wailing and tears are more appropriate to the ambience.

As if sensing that joy violates some prevailing standard of decorum, Paul repeats himself. *"I will say it again: Rejoice!"* Joy, which takes pleasure in goodness and holiness and fine fellowship, is in itself pleasurable. When joy rises to the surface, the joyful rejoice in the joy, which then increases all the more.

I became aware of this proliferating effect of joy recently. Through some fluke of scheduling (or the kindness of my secretary), I remained in Calgary an extra day following a speaking assignment for the Western Canada Christian Convention. My hosts were Allan and Judy Dunbar, longtime friends to whom God has given the gift of hospitality, among their many abilities. To climax a restful, refreshing day together, Allan and Judy took me to Calgary's Jack Singer Auditorium for Diane Bish's magnificent organ concert. Allan is an accomplished organist, able to listen with an appreciation for nuances that escaped Judy and me. We simply absorbed the beauty of the music and were awed by Miss Bish's technical mastery of the instrument. All of us enthusiastically applauded at the concert's close, calling the organist back for more. We wanted an encore. She didn't disappoint.

Something happened during the applause. We had clapped, of course, for each of her numbers (especially the Bach pieces), but at the end we outdid ourselves in expressing our joy in her performance. Later I realized that while I had thoroughly "enjoyed" the concert, my joy was doubled during the ovation.

Lewis Smedes says something similar happened to him at an Isaac Stern violin concert. He, too, felt even greater joy in the ovation than in the concert. And he knew why. "I had felt the goodness of Stern's gift and was giving freely of my gift in return. And I knew that this experience was a paradigm of human joy in a life given by a loving Creator."[6]

God gives, and we are thankful. But when we give thanks in return for his giving, our thanksgiving doubles the gladness we feel.

So we rejoice. And rejoice that we can rejoice.

It is glory enough for me
That I should be Your servant
It is grace enough for me
That You should be my Lord.[7]

"Let your gentleness be evident to all"

Consider the synonyms of gentleness: *sensitivity, appreciation, consideration, kindness, tenderness, sympathy, perceptiveness, temperateness, delicacy, civilized demeanor.*

There's nothing wimpy about gentleness. In Paul's order of things here, it is the natural consequence of a joyful life. He seems to be suggesting something like this: If you will *rejoice* in the Lord, really rejoice *in the Lord*, and you will do it *always*, that is, in every circumstance and under all conditions, even those that seem against you, you will not treat other people competitively nor with hostility. Instead you will view them as you perceive yourself, persons whom the Lord loves. Since you are the Lord's, you will as a matter of course be gentle with all others he has made.

You will not harbor anger against another. You will not get even, though you have been wronged. You will forgive, as hard as it may be to do so. You will not succumb to or be guided by this world's distorted value system. Screwtape can't get you.

The ability to be gentle toward all doesn't come easily. Probably the best primer on the subject is Jesus' Sermon on the Mount, specifically the Beatitudes. Max Lucado helped me to hear Jesus with keener ears in his *Applause of Heaven*. He calls attention to the sequence in Matthew 5.

First, we recognize we are in need (we're poor in spirit).
Next, we repent of our self-sufficiency (we mourn).
We quit calling the shots and surrender control to God (we're meek).
So grateful are we for his presence that we yearn for more of him (we hunger and thirst).
As we grow closer to him, we become more like him. We forgive others (we're merciful).
We change our outlook (we're pure in heart).
We love others (we're peacemakers).
We endure injustice (we're persecuted).

"It's no casual shift of attitude," Lucado warns. "It is a demolition of the old structure and a creation of the new. *The more radical the change, the greater the joy.* And it's worth every effort, for this is the joy of God."[8]

What is the essence of the change? It is the voluntary putting aside of one's despotic ego in favor of Christ's always-giving Spirit. Paul expresses it best: "I have been crucified with Christ and I no longer live, but Christ lives in me" (Galatians 2:20). From rejoicing in and for oneself to rejoicing in the Lord. Always.

"The Lord is near"

Here is the reason for the gaiety. You are not alone. The Lord is at hand.

In the context of the apostle's ministry, this simple statement may allude to one of Paul's favorite themes, the imminent return of the Lord. The conclusion of Philippians 3 argues for this interpretation:

> But our citizenship is in heaven. And we eagerly await a Savior from there, the Lord Jesus Christ, who, by the power that enables him to bring everything under his control, will transform our lowly bodies so that they will be like his glorious body.

The immediate paragraph that surrounds it, however, points to the comforting presence of the Lord's spirit. He is near, at hand, and because he is,

> Do not be anxious about anything, but in everything, by prayer and petition, with thanksgiving, present your requests to God.

The Lord is near. You do not need to be anxious, just prayerful.

> We mutter and sputter;
> We fume and we spurt;
> We mumble and grumble;
> Our feelings get hurt.
>
> We can't understand things;
> Our vision grows dim,
> When all that we need
> Is a moment with him.[9]

Jesus' occasional retreats to the mountains gave him that "moment with him." Of course, the Father was always with him, when the crowd was crushing and his ministrations were enervating, but he knew the special power of the retreat, when he could be alone with the Father. Philip Wiebe waggishly assures us that when Jesus took his retreats, "he wasn't heading off for the latest Rabbi Retreat featuring 'The Day's Most Dynamic Communicators' along with 'The Finest in Contemporary Jewish Music.'"[10] We don't need to ask what Wiebe thinks of today's loudly-hyped pastors' seminars! Jesus' retreats were, instead, escapes from hype to touch base again with the heavenly, to listen, to be still, to know that God is God.

From the conviction that the Lord is near, then, comes deliverance from anxiety and confidence in prayer. And that's not all.

And the peace of God, which transcends all understanding, will guard your hearts and your minds in Christ Jesus.

There's that "in Christ Jesus," again. This peace that Paul promises is not a blank check to be filled in quickly and cashed. He doesn't promise the peace of God if you'll "only believe" in a higher power of some kind. Paul addresses his words to very particular persons: those *in* Christ Jesus. No generic religiosity will satisfy. This isn't faith in faith that he is propagating. The rejoicing, he insists, will be "in the Lord." You can rest assured "the Lord is near." You can "present your requests to God." And you can receive the "peace of God . . . in Christ Jesus."

There's something refreshing about Paul's Christ-centeredness. Living in a religiously pluralistic era, we are forced in public gatherings to listen to a lot of pseudo-prayers uttered by compromised pray-ers. Not wanting to offend, even well-intentioned Christians sometimes deny the essence of their faith as they pray. Duke chaplain William Willimon reports on the time he heard a minister offer the invocation at a community gathering, "Great One, source of all being, immerse in the human

163

condition. Amen." Willimon was seated next to Bible scholar Walter Brueggemann, who muttered at the end of the prayer, 'Lord, this is Walt. I don't want any more immersion in the human condition than I've already got.'"[11]

Amen! What we want is immersion in Christ. We're awash to our eyeballs in the human condition and we need help. So we are asking for it. Henry Van Dyke says it better than I can:

> These are the gifts I ask
> Of Thee, Spirit serene:
> Strength for the daily task,
> Courage to face the road,
> Good cheer to help me bear the traveller's load,
> And, for the hours of rest that come between,
> *An inward joy* in all things heard and seen.
>
> These are the sins I fain
> Would have thee take away:
> Malice, and cold disdain,
> Hot anger, sullen hate,
> Scorn of the lowly, envy of the great,
> And discontent that casts a shadow gray
> On all the brightness of the common day.[12]

I also like the famous Breton fishermen's prayer:

> Dear God, be good to me;
> The sea is so wide,
> And my boat is so small.

Such prayers are possible when you believe "the Lord is near."

Think On These

Finally, brothers, whatever is true, whatever is noble, whatever is right, whatever is pure, whatever is lovely, whatever is admirable—if anything is excellent or praiseworthy—think about such things.

These verses are both cause and effect. If you learn to "think about such things," your spirits will be lifted to the height of your thoughts, and rejoicing will naturally follow. Conversely, if you obey Paul's injunction and learn to "rejoice in the Lord always," your thoughts will rise in time to the height of your joy. The best counsel, then, is to do both at once: rejoice and think thoughts that are true, noble, right, pure, lovely, admirable. Be high minded *and* high spirited.

Could Paul have had Psalm 51:10-12 in mind as he wrote?

Create in me a pure heart, O God,
　　[*let your gentleness be evident*]
and renew a steadfast spirit within me.
　　[*Do not be anxious about anything*]
Do not cast me from your presence
or take your Holy Spirit from me.
　　[*The Lord is near*]
Restore to me the *joy* of your salvation
　　[*Rejoice in the Lord always*]
and grant me a willing spirit, to sustain me.
　　[*He will guard your hearts and minds in Christ Jesus*]

Paul returns in the eighth verse to the great hymn of chapter two: "Your attitude," he says, "should be the same as that of Christ Jesus." It's stronger in the King James Version: "Let this mind be in you, which was also in Christ Jesus. . . ." Such a mind thinks thoughts that are true, noble, right, pure, lovely, and admirable.

Ellen Charry in the "Moral Function of Doctrine," must have been reading Paul's Philippian letter just before she wrote,

Christians are not self-creations but creatures bound by God and one another; their behavior, attitudes, and striving take shape within those boundaries. *Christians are not alone in the world, and they do not have to invent the means for attaining their happiness.* Thus, from a practical vantage point, dogmatic theology and the church that it sustains turn out to be *a therapeutic community for those who hitch their wagon to the Lord's star.*

You have to admit that "dogmatic theology" is pretty serious business. So is the church. Yet Ms. Charry uses words like *not alone, happiness,* and *therapeutic* when discussing this serious business. Could she be right? And could C. S. Lewis, quoted earlier, who thought *joy* the *serious business* of Heaven? If they are right, and they are, then what's a Christian to do but rejoice?

Always.

---

[1]*Leaving Home.* New York: Penguin, 1987, p. xv.

[2]Graham Greene, *Ways of Escape.* New York: Simon and Schuster, 1980, p. 10.

[3]Quoted in John Winokur, *The Portable Curmudgeon.* New York: New American Library, 1987, p. 173.

[4]Charles P. Curtis, *A Commonplace Book.* New York: Simon and Schuster, 1957, p. 206.

[5]C. S. Lewis, *Screwtape Letters,* quoted in *Christianity Today,* February 7, 1986, p. 16. Italics mine.

[6]Lewis Smedes, *Mere Morality.* Grand Rapids: Eerdmans, 1983, pp. 125, 126.

[7]An Arabic Prayer in George Appleton, *The Oxford Book of Prayer.* New York: Oxford University, 1985, p. 332.

[8]Max Lucado, *The Applause of Heaven.* Dallas: Word, 1990, p. 12. Italics mine.

[9]Author unknown.

[10]Philip Wiebe in *The Christian Leader,* April 9, 1991; quoted in *Christianity Today,* November 11, 1991, p. 33.

[11]Quoted in Martin Marty, *Context,* June 1, 1992, pp. 1, 2.

[12]Reproduced in Leslie D. Weatherhead, *A Private House of Prayer.* New York: Abingdon, 1958, p. 169.

Chapter 12

On Becoming a Good Cheerleader

Hebrews 12:1, 2

When asked what I like best about being a minister, I have a ready answer. As you can probably tell from my writing, I like just about everything about pastoral ministry. It is a privileged calling, with greater rewards than most people can imagine. Ours never makes the list of the best paid professions, but money would be the least of our rewards anyway, even if we earned what professional athletes or entertainers make. Our real pay comes in other ways. What do I like best? I get to watch people grow. And not only watch—I get to help. Nothing is more fun than celebrating the successful achievement of someone in whom we have invested ourselves. This is true especially of those whom we are preparing to continue our work after we are gone.

A pastor's joy is the multiplied pleasure of a parent. My wife Joy and I shepherded our three children to maturity. They are adults now, on their own, struggling with career decisions and budgets and children, just as we did. When they stumble, we grieve; when they succeed, we cheer. When they ask for help, we give it to them if we can.

As ministers, we have shepherded many other people's children toward *Christian* maturity. Some of our spiritual children are on mission fields, others in leadership roles in churches, still others making a positive difference in their communities, in their businesses, and in their family lives. We glory in their accomplishments. We cheer them on. They are not aware how much joy they bring us.

Cheering is a role for which high school prepared me. Unable to be on the playing field because of uncertain health and very certain physical ineptitude, I was early confined to the bleachers. I would have preferred playing; in my school if you weren't a jock, you weren't a man! But since I couldn't be one, I made the best of the situation and took in every football and basketball game our school played, yelling myself hoarse, trying by sheer personal willpower to push our team to victory.

We had regular pep rallies at Tillamook High. Mr. Hornback, the principal, dismissed classes so the whole student body could assemble in the gymnasium, where coaches and players tried their motivational best to whip up enthusiasm for the evening's game, and the cheerleaders rehearsed the yells we would be shouting during the contest. We left the rallies hyped up for the big events. The purpose of the rallies, evident to all of us, was to persuade everybody that every person, every voice, was needed to cheer our players on to victory. The athletes couldn't do it alone. They needed our support.

What I learned in high school I've continued in the ministry. Cheering others on is a pastor's vocation.

A Host of Cheerleaders

The writer of Hebrews urges us to run our race with perseverance, since there is a host of saints in eternity's stadium cheering us on. Gordon MacDonald calls them "a crowd of retired athletes," men and women who ran by faith and didn't quit. "The world was not worthy of them," Hebrews 11:38 says. MacDonald finds himself "both fascinated and not a little anxious over the fact that they are sitting in that grandstand watching me."[1]

They don't make me anxious. Although they see what a poor spiritual specimen I am, they will have more sympathy for my plight than someone who has never run the race. They know the required discipline, the early humiliations, the frequent setbacks, the occasional taste of success followed by occasional slumps and frustrating plateaus. They know also how elusive is the perfection any serious competitor, especially one in a spiritual contest, strives to achieve. I am cheered by their sympathy and encouraged by their example.

At my present stage in life and ministry, I don't have too many more years before my place will no longer be on the track. The time is rapidly approaching when I'll climb the steps to sit in the stands beside them, and not as a dumb spectator, either. Having been helped by so many who've gone before me, I will imitate them, doing everything I can to cheer on those who will be running in my place.

At a recent state ministers' retreat, I became aware of something I had never seen before. Larry Hostetler, my colleague who serves the Chaparral Christian Church in Scottsdale, was there. When our family first moved to Arizona, we became acquainted with Larry, an outstanding young minister. In our time together I've come to appreciate his steady, quality work in his congregation and on behalf of the whole state. But when I saw him at the retreat, what came to mind was not his leadership role but his age. We are contemporaries. "Larry, do you realize you and I are the oldest persons here?"

For so many years I had been accustomed to being one of the youngest at any gathering of ministers. I wasn't psychologically prepared for my new role. Senior statesman. Experienced counselor. Old head. Say it any way you want, it still sounds like "almost over the hill."

My role is changing, but I am without regrets. Nothing now is more important than cheering on the younger runners.

Sharon Sterrenburg wrote an open letter to Pastor Dan Blied of the Whittier Hills Baptist Church in California. For six years Sharon had been a member of his staff. She wrote not only to thank him for his leadership but to share her analysis of why staff relationships at Whittier Hills Baptist had been so productive. She listed seven reasons:

1) I had a well-defined job.
2) I had good resources from the start.
3) I had a team [the women she worked with and the church staff].
4) I had regular encouragement.
5) I had someone who believed in me.
6) I had a role model.
7) I had good leadership.[2]

What stands out in her list is the crucial role encouragement plays. She mentions it specifically only once, but it is implicit in several other items: "good resources," "team," "someone who believed in me," "good leadership." When Sharon joined the staff, she was not abandoned to failure. Her boss cared enough to give her detailed, specific instructions concerning her responsibilities. He provided what she needed for success. He surrounded her with fellow workers so she didn't have to go it alone. He modeled what she should be, he led her where she should go, he let her know he believed in her.

That's good cheerleading. You can hear the same concern in Paul's letters to the young Christians he shepherded:

For you know that we dealt with each of you as a father deals with his own children, encouraging, comforting, and urging you to live lives worthy of God, who calls you into his kingdom and glory (1 Thessalonians 2:11, 12).

And in Jesus' encouragement to his tired disciples:

Come to me, all you who are weary and burdened, and I will give you rest. Take my yoke upon you and learn from me, for I am gentle and humble in heart, and you will find rest for your souls. For my yoke is easy and my burden is light (Matthew 11:28-30).

Jesus doesn't take the burden away, but he shares the load and teaches a better way.

That wonderful compendium of wisdom, the Book of Proverbs, speaks of the cheerleader's effect:

An anxious heart weighs a man down,
but a kind word cheers him up (Proverbs 12:25).

A man finds joy in giving an apt reply—
and how good is a timely word! (Proverbs 15:23).

Pleasant words are a honeycomb,
sweet to the soul and healing to the bones (Proverbs 16:24).

A cheerful look brings joy to the heart,
and good news gives health to the bones (Proverbs 15:30).

What occupation can be more rewarding, what vocation can show more immediate results, than the cheerleader's? Who else can so effectively lift "an anxious heart" and bring "healing to the bones," and find such joy in the process?

A Helping Mentor

Cheerleaders connotes crowds, groups. It *is* possible to gain great encouragement from speakers addressing crowds, like those at the pep rally. Frequently a letter comes from someone I've never met, someone in a crowd somewhere, to tell me that something I have said has given courage to keep on. Reading the letter makes me feel like the man who "finds joy in giving an apt reply." The cheerleader is cheered.

Here is an excerpt from a letter that I received awhile ago.

171

. . . there seemed to be times that the church emptied and you were speaking directly to me. This happens often when I attend your services. I believe that it was God that spoke to me and directed that I go inside to your services. . . . I want God in my life, and I seek his guidance, but I fear that I do not know enough about him. . . .

The writer provided his telephone number, and in a few days he and his wife were visiting with me. They are well on their way toward a rich new life in the Lord. They were introduced to him through worship and sermon. They received the encouragement to return for more teaching. They really do want to learn. My role now is to cheer them on.

In this instance, I had two privileges: 1) giving the "speech at the pep rally," and 2) moving into a more personal relationship with them. In the second sense, I am more mentor than cheerleader. The term *mentor* has been appropriated by the business world; its religious equivalent is *discipler,* a term I'm avoiding here because it is too specific. It suggests a more hands-on approach to encouraging another's growth than I want to propose. In fact, in the wrong hands, the whole concept of discipling can be easily abused; it becomes the justification for mind control and psychological tyranny, of which there has been too much in the religious world.

A mentor does not assume responsibility for his protege's total being. Continuing the business analogy, the mentor is an adviser, a guide through the labyrinth of corporate culture, a teacher to an apprentice who observes, questions, and follows. The mentor makes suggestions concerning life outside of business, but he recognizes his limits. His primary responsibility is helping the student to do his job well, well enough that he can, one day, stand independent of, and even replace, the mentor.

A special 1983 edition of *The Harvard Business Review* carried an article entitled "Everyone Who Makes It Has a

Mentor." In it F. J. Lunding of Jewel Companies, appointed successor to the famous John Hancock, shares his "first assistant" philosophy, the belief that executive responsibility involves assisting the people down the line to be successful. The boss in any department is the first assistant to those who report to him. Lunding passed his philosophy on to his successor George Clements, who handed it on to his handpicked successor Donald Perkins, who likens this sponsorship to parenthood. He says, "I don't know that anyone has ever succeeded in any business without having some unselfish sponsorship or mentorship, whatever it might be called.[3]

Unselfish sponsorship. Doesn't this sound very much like Barnabas's protection and nurture of Saul of Tarsus? (See Acts 9:26-30.) Or Paul's sponsorship of Timothy? (See 1 and 2 Timothy.) Or Jesus' mentoring of his twelve disciples?

In Robert Coleman's very popular book, *The Master Plan of Evangelism,* the author analyzes Jesus' method of calling and preparing his disciples to succeed him in ministry. The components are

(1) selection
(2) association
(3) concentration
(4) impartation
(5) demonstration
(6) delegation
(7) supervision
(8) reproduction.[4]

You and I might challenge Coleman on some particulars of his analysis, but we would agree that he has the order and the method right. Jesus poured himself into his men, giving them all they needed to be his successors in ministry, even encouraging them to believe they would be able to do more than he was doing. (See John 14:12.)

A Hopeful Waymaker

Using Jesus as an example is a little misleading, since he forever remains mentor, discipler, master, and lord. He will not be succeeded.

The rest of us will. Our role will be more like that of John the Baptist, who made a way in the wilderness for his Lord. "He must increase," John said of Jesus. "I must decrease." John's appointed role in history was to prepare the way of the Lord. Having done that, he fades from the story.

Our appointed roles as Christian leaders are likewise to prepare the way for the Lord to come to people, and for people to come to the Lord. Further, we must prepare the way for the one coming after us, making our successor's climb easier, indicating the dangers, pointing to the source of help.

For the last few years I have been praying and thinking a great deal about my successors, first at the church and more recently at the college. I am keenly aware of the perils of transition. Many fine churches have collapsed because the pastor gave no thought to succession. Having no authority to name our successors, many of us wash our hands of all responsibility. We fail to select and train an apprentice. We think we are too busy with our nearly overwhelming responsibilities to take time to cheer another upward. In the end, we leave our churches in a cheerless condition.

We must appear to think we are immortal. Denying death or decrepitude, we make no provision for the future. We act as if we plan to stay in the saddle forever. We probably ought to take George Washington as our model. Our country has produced no more effective leader. His legacy lives on. Whenever his achievements are extolled, one of the chief accolades is for the manner in which he left office. He could have reigned until he died. Instead he is honored today as our Cincinnatus. Like the Roman general called from his fields to assume command of his nation's army and then returned to his fields when war was over, Washington returned to Mt. Vernon when his second term ended. It was time for another to increase; he must decrease.

We honor Washington because we have found his humility rare in public life. Usually one who increases likes to keep on increasing. Rare is the leader who recognizes when it is time to turn things over to his successor, and then cheer him or her on.

A Heavenly Model

Let's return to the Lord. The writer of Hebrews exhorts us to look to Jesus, "the author and perfecter of our faith." Look to him as one singlemindedly fixed on the goal he wished to achieve; look to him who endured the cross for the sake of reaching the goal; and look to him who now sits in the privileged position with God. Look to him "so that you will not grow weary and lose heart."

Looking to him who "endured such opposition from sinful men," we are reminded that "in all these things we are more than conquerors through him who loved us." "If God is for us, who can be against us?" (Romans 8:37, 31).

Look to him not so much for his encouraging words, though he spoke many, but for his encouraging character. Just to know him and to know you belong to someone like him is an encouragement. You may not agree with me at first, because Jesus seems so unlike other role models. He isn't rich, politically powerful, macho, or heroic in any media-capturing way. He has often been characterized, even by his admirers, as something of a clown or madman, since he is so much at odds with what this world admires.

Some people took genuine offense when they learned that Norman Lear modeled *All in the Family*'s Edith Bunker on Jesus. "We always thought Edith would react to things exactly the way Jesus would. She's somebody who swallowed the Sermon on the Mount and lived it.

And that was always our guideline for Edith."[5] The *American Family Association Journal* was incensed.

> Edith, the character whom Lear identified as reacting as Jesus would, was an addle-brained, absent-minded, naive woman who never knew what was going on. She was a simpleton whose family and friends had simply learned to endure her. Whenever she proposed moral principles or Biblical ideas, she was quickly and totally overruled by her bigoted husband.

Yes, she was. But it was Archie, not Edith, who was the object of the series' satire. Even casual viewers like me knew that when Edith spoke, she would speak honestly, kindly, and self-sacrificially. She was always my favorite *All in the Family* character. If I were ever in need, it would be Edith and never Archie that I'd send for.

A young theologian once asserted that the Christian thought of God has always had mystery at its center. His wiser companion amended his judgment: "No. The Christian thought of God has always had mystery at its periphery. But at its center, the face of Jesus Christ."

Exactly.

And what a Jesus. He presents himself, this all-time champion leader and model, not as a wielder of power but as a servant of servants. "In this world you will have trouble," he said. "But take heart! I have overcome the world," he said (John 16:33). His method of overcoming, however, defies the counsel of worldly politics. Without resort to subterfuge or media blitzes or power moves, he defeated Satan and rescued humanity. His method was as simple as his motive was pure: he merely pushed his love to the extreme. He conquered with a cross. He made it possible for all who believe in him to find forgiveness, to experience a new start.

My friend Bob Russell, long an ardent sports enthusiast, says that one of his favorite moments in NCAA basketball came during a tournament game between

Georgetown and North Carolina. The score was tied with only twelve seconds remaining in the game. Out of the corner of his eye, Freddie Brown of Georgetown saw a player he mistook for a teammate. He threw him the ball, but a North Carolina player caught it, ran to the other end, and scored. Georgetown lost the game. When the final buzzer sounded, television cameras focused on Georgetown's six-foot-ten-inch Coach John Thompson as he embraced Freddie Brown in a big bear hug. Wise man. "A word of encouragement during a failure is worth more than a whole book of praise after success."[6]

A good coach is one third mentor, one third model, and one third cheerleader.

Once you have taken the cheerleader's part and have tasted the sheer pleasure of rooting enthusiastically for others, though you can no longer take to the field, you'll discover there is something even more satisfying than earning the winner's crown yourself. Winning the race or being voted Most Valuable Player or holding the victor's cup is a sometime thing. You bask in your moment of glory, place your trophy on the shelf, and forever point back to the time when you were somebody. It felt good at the time, and it feels good in remembrance, but only good.

Cheering, on the other hand, is unfettered by time. Year after year, for player after player, you can yell your praise. When you are old you can't play any more, but when you are old, as long as you have breath, you can cheer. Old athletes can't make the team, but old cheerleaders are always welcome in the stadium. When the game is over, and the contestant has given his all, where does he look? To the stands, to a certain section of the stands, where he knows he'll find his cheerleader. He has been playing for her, giving his all for him.

That's the paradox of it all. When you are focusing your attention out there, yelling and praying and hoping and vicariously playing with your successor, the object of your attention and affection is doing everything possible to please you. Then you who have forgotten yourself for the sake of another gain the greatest reward.

Blessed indeed is the cheerleader, for he shall find celebration without end.

---

[1]Gordon MacDonald, *Christ Followers in the Real World.* Nashville: Oliver Nelson, 1991, p. 19.

[2]Sharon Sterrenburg, "What Makes a Staff Succeed?" *Leadership,* Fall 1990, p. 69.

[3]Bruce W. Jones, *Ministerial Leadership in a Mangerial World.* Wheaton: Tyndale House, 1988, p. 31.

[4]Jones, *Ministerial Leadership*, p. 30.

[5]Quoted in an article in *American Family Association Journal,* April 1991, pp. 1, 21.

[6]Bob Russell, *Take Comfort.* Cincinnati: Standard, 1991, p. 133.

Chapter 13

Our Regular Weekly Party

Luke 22:14-23

This book was very much on my mind in June of 1992, when my companions and I were touring Scandinavia. Every day was filled with unforgettable vistas and involuntary praises. God does good work! By late afternoon one day we had observed about as much beauty as we could absorb. Cresting one hill, after gasping and shrieking through the hairpin curves, we came upon a panorama of almost paralyzing magnificence. "I'm experiencing sensory overload," I told my companion. "I don't think I can take in any more." Mike Prior felt the same. "It is hard to sleep with all this incessant scenery."

Although it was mid-summer, the longest day of Norway's nightless season, a brisk breeze reminded us we were far north. Arizona was never like this. Our tour photographers were trying their best to capture the startling contrast between the deep blue fjord below and the snow-covered mountains around us. They couldn't, and they knew they couldn't. Their relatives would never know what they were seeing and feeling. Some experiences won't communicate. You have to have been there.

Then came the stop at the Hopperstad Stave Church in Vik. Our guide told us that, though it was not the most famous of the country's 29 extant ones (of the more than one thousand that once were), he really wanted us to see it. He himself was Danish, but he loved this bit of Norwegian heritage. "Stave" refers to the upright pine pillars that support the entire structure; the walls merely "hang" from them. The entire building is of specially prepared pine. First, the tree was shorn of limbs while still rooted in the ground. When it had dried sufficiently it was cut down, smoothed, and set alongside others in its consecrated place.

The stave churches are centuries old, the one we visited dating back to A.D. 1150. They were fashioned by the same craftsmen who built the Viking ships, the ceiling looking much like the ship's hull, but upside down. Only a little light enters through the tiny windows up high.

There are no seats. The country was Catholic then, and people stood. The men entered through the main door; women and children came in through an opening on the side. Only the priest used the door in the altar area. A small covered walkway surrounded the building on three sides. That was for the lepers, who dared not enter the sanctuary. They could stand outside, though, and listen.

No one used the leper's walk the day we were there. A handful of other tourists walked in, poked about a bit, and left. They could see that something special was happening with us.

And it was. We had paused for worship. Gary Tiffin led us in a Communion meditation from Revelation, where the saints are gathered before the throne praising the One who is worthy. He called attention to the worthies who had labored to erect this house of worship so many centuries ago. We had something in common with them. He reminded us of our loved ones back in America who would, in just a few minutes, be leaving for early church services. He had us meditate on our connection with the future, as well. One day people would be thinking back on our era.

Then we sang a couple of songs and partook of Communion. Nick, our Danish guide, had secured the grape juice and rolls for the occasion, a satisfactory substitute, we felt. The little individual cups some American churches have come to think essential to the observance were missing as well. We had only a single goblet, so we dipped the bread, a silent coupling with worshipers centuries past and present for whom the tincture method is commonplace.

It became very still. I don't know what others were thinking or praying. My mind thought of home. Mark Chitwood would begin preaching the early-bird service in just half an hour. Church service would be conducted as usual, but this time without me. Then I thought again of the centuries of Christian worship that had occurred in this simple building, humble people coming week by week to hear and commune and be blessed. Now here we were, tourists on a jaunt, contributing nothing to Norway but our tourist dollars, receiving so much more in beauty than we could ever pay for. I took the bread and the cup, again receiving so much more than I could pay for. And I quietly rejoiced.

In the stillness we celebrated. The cup was handed from person to person. Nick, our ever-gracious guide, wouldn't have it any other way. He personally passed out the little loaves, and our worshipers, knowing he was not in any denominational sense "one of us," graciously let him, for in his serving was he not more like the One who took the towel and wash basin to serve his disciples than we who simply stood and received? And did it not speak eloquently of Communion's meaning, this being served by one for whom Scandinavia is home? We were his guests as well as the Lord's, and he welcomed us.

When we departed, we were subdued though very satisfied. We had prayed. We had sung. We had touched the ancients and given thanks for them. We had remembered our contemporaries, and asked God's blessing on them. We had thought of the future, when we shall be gone from this planet and remembered by only a few. And we had joined for the moment Revelation's singing saints at the throne of the Lamb. It felt good to have been there.

We had reached back two thousand years. Some parties are for remembering: Christmas, Easter, Memorial Day, Thanksgiving, Independence Day, Veterans Day, Martin Luther King Day. Special days, so we won't forget.

At first, a simple meal, then, gradually, something more complicated. After the collapse of Rome, liturgical confusion was widespread throughout what had been the empire. In many places orderly worship virtually disappeared, while in other places widely varying rites were used for different reasons. In time the emergent kings of France and successive bishops of Rome were drawn into political alliance, until on Christmas Day A.D. 800, Pope Leo crowned Charlemagne Emperor in Rome. The new Emperor vowed to restore the Roman liturgy throughout his realm and commissioned Alcuin, master of the cathedral school in York, to effect the restoration.

Alcuin brought to his work the zeal and integrity of a scrupulous scholar. As a result, the Roman mass, with only minor local variations, was adopted throughout western Europe. For the next seven hundred years it survived, but profound changes occurred in the way it was performed until the Reformers of the sixteenth century adopted radical, even revolutionary, variations.

In the earlier centuries, the eucharistic table, which had once stood in the center of the worshiping congregation and had then been moved towards the eastern end of the building, was moved so close to the east wall that it became impossible for the celebrant to stand behind it. He was forced to stand in front of the table with his back to the people. At the same time, the table, which had originally been made of wood, became one of stone and to take on more and more the appearance of an altar. From about 1100 onwards, in Rome, candles were placed on the table, and a hundred years later, a crucifix. Further adornments were added during the late medieval period.

All these changes enhanced the role of the priest. Instead of being the president of the worshiping and communicating people of God, he became an intermediary acting on their behalf. Not only did the priest celebrate the eucharist with his back to the people, but a massive rood screen was built across the end of the chancel in nearly every church, keeping the people in the nave away from the priest and thus away from active participation in the eucharistic action. Not surprisingly, the decline in lay Communion, which had begun in the fourth century after the accession of Constantine, now gained momentum. For if the bread and wine became the actual body and blood of Christ, as was now the dogma of the church, who was worthy to handle and receive? The people went to watch, and only occasionally, perhaps three times a year, to receive the bread, while the wine was reserved for the priest alone. Thus the note of joyful thanksgiving in the eucharist, so evident in the New Testament and in the early centuries of the church's life, was replaced with an atmosphere of fear and awe. In time the host itself was worshiped.

Monastic priests, too numerous to be able to preside over the celebration of the eucharist with any regularity, began holding private masses. That, in turn, led to the practice of "votive masses," masses said to secure private blessings. As early as 694 a synod at Toledo had had to condemn the practice of saying masses to bring about someone's death! Still, the votive mass became integral to the medieval religious system. Simple Communion, a means of corporate thanksgiving for blessings from Christ, had evolved into a private means of securing private blessings. Because priests charged for these private masses, the supposed benefits were more readily available to the rich than to the poor; they could afford to pay.[1]

What a long way the simple meal the first Christians enjoyed had come by the sixteenth century. For the early Christians, the meal wasn't anything mysterious; it was simply something their Lord had asked them to do when they met together, an expression of their faith, gratitude, and shared life in Christ.

To Remember

"Do this in memory of me," he had said. So they did. And so we do.

Not long ago I spoke to a group of high school students visiting the Pacific Christian College campus. They had been invited to look the campus over, the college hoping they would choose to enroll after their high school graduation. The organizing committee asked me to say a few words of welcome and challenge.

I don't know what came over me, but when I looked at their young faces the subject I could not stifle was funerals. I asked the young people to imagine they had just died at sixty and the family had called me in to preach their funeral. What would they like to have me say? High school students, if they think of death at all, usually believe it's for someone else. They are exempt. They have "intimations of immortality," as Wordsworth would say, and honestly can't imagine themselves dead. And here was the college president asking them what he should say at their funerals!

My goal was to help them decide, even in their teens, what they would like to be remembered for after they are gone. I probably succeeded only in confusing them and causing them to wonder about this doddering old man.

It's a generally fair question, though, isn't it? Certainly it was on Jesus' mind that evening in the upper room when he transformed a simple meal into a memorial service. "Do this in remembrance of me." Remember his body, given like the broken bread, for their sakes. Remember his blood, poured out on their behalf. Remember the new covenant established by his sacrifice. Remember that, even in that intimate circle, a traitor existed, so as the apostle Paul counseled, "a man ought to examine himself before he eats of the bread and drinks of the cup" (1 Corinthians 11:28). Remember that who you were you are to be no longer.

In spite of Jesus' direct instructions, remembering him nearly died out in the Middle Ages. In Rome, for example, of the 433 churches and chapels, only 15 were dedicated to Jesus. No fewer than 121 were dedicated to his mother. According to Harold Fey, "Ignatius Loyola and some other medieval Catholics even went so far as to teach that in the Eucharist the flesh of Mary as well as that of Jesus was eaten."[2]

Many churches today have restored the early Christian practice of observing Communion at least every week. Ours is one of them. What I like best as a preacher is that no matter what my specific sermon topic is, no one can attend worship in our church without remembering Jesus in the breaking of the bread and the sharing of the cup.

To Recommit, Realign

"This cup is the new covenant in my blood. . . ." A covenant is an agreement, a treaty, a mutual commitment binding the covenanting parties to fulfill the terms of the contract. For centuries the Jews had lived under the Mosaic covenant. Now Jesus was ushering in a new one from God to his people, one bought by the blood of the Lamb of God. Those covered by this agreement have the promise of forgiven sins and full acceptance as sons and daughters of the Father. Their part of the agreement is their grateful acceptance of the grace offered and sacrifice of themselves, "living sacrifices, holy and pleasing to God," not conformed to this world and unhampered by conceit (Romans 12:1-3).

Psychiatrist Scott Peck tells of working with a woman who, he said, "had a strange terror of taking communion." He accurately diagnosed her problem as pride. After some work on it, her terror "almost magically disappeared." When she mentioned she'd been to church the preceding Sunday, he asked whether she'd taken Communion. "No," she admitted.

"I thought you'd gotten over your fear of it."

"Oh, I have. It doesn't bother me at all now."

"Then why didn't you take it Sunday?"

"I just didn't feel like it that morning.

"You didn't feel like it?"

"Yes, I didn't feel like it."

Dr. Peck then, as he said, "lit into her." He decided she needed to learn the meaning of Communion.

> When Jesus let himself be nailed to the cross that Friday morning, when he was strung up and his muscles began to go all into spasm, when he allowed his body to be broken for you, do you think he *felt* like it?

By definition, Peck explained, sacrifice is not something we feel like. "If it felt easy, fun, good, then it wouldn't be a sacrifice. . . ."

In time, when we understand what we are doing, Communion brings joy and good feeling. But in the beginning, it feels like sacrifice, especially the sacrifice of pride. "We must first admit that we need Jesus."

So Dr. Peck asked his patient,

> Did you ever think that maybe it isn't a question of whether you feel like taking communion or not? That whether or not you feel like it, maybe you need it? That maybe you are lost and lonely even when you don't feel lost and lonely? And that Jesus longs for you to come to him, and that by sitting smugly in your pew you are disappointing him? That he needs you? That just maybe you have an obligation to sacrifice yourself for him as he sacrificed himself for you?[3]

Each week the Lord's Supper affords us the opportunity to realign ourselves to his will, to recommit ourselves to renewed diligence, and to reaffirm our faith.

To Appreciate

"After taking the cup, he gave thanks. . . ."

"And he took bread, gave thanks and broke it. . . ."

This is the reason Communion came to be called "the eucharist," for the word means "thanksgiving." Actually, it means more. *Eu*: good, well; *charis*: favor, grace. The

186

eucharist, then, is the believers' way of acknowledging the special grace God has given us through Christ, and to acknowledge such a great gift is to give thanks.

We come to the table in humble appreciation, then, almost in awe. What believer could not identify with the rugged miner Robert Hicks tells of. Hicks says one of the most memorable Communion services he ever experienced was held in the Australian outback. There was no pastor, so the men of the church took turns leading. The day Hicks visited was the miner's turn. He held all his noted index cards in his hand. In the middle of the ceremony, he dropped all of them. Trying to regain his composure, he attempted to put the cards back in order. The stress was too great. He started crying. "I wanted to do such a good job for the Lord." Robert Hicks said there wasn't a dry eye in the place. "Isn't this what Communion is all about," he asks, "bringing our brokenness to the brokenness of Christ and finding the acceptance and forgiveness we so need in him?"[4]

So we give thanks for the Lord.

And for one another in the Lord. I prefer the word *communion* to *eucharist,* not only because I'm basically "low church" but because *communion* underscores the truth that the Lord's Supper was not intended by our Lord to be a solitary experience. Communion is a common meal, with shared bread and wine. Paul had to scold the Corinthian Christians because, in their selfishness, they were not looking after one another properly. (See 1 Corinthians 11.) Sometimes we deserve a similar reprimand.

While in Manila to address the Filipino International Christian Convention a few months ago, I attended a session for leaders. An elder spoke from the floor of an exciting event in his church. One Saturday thirty converts became a part of their fellowship through baptism. The next day being Sunday, the leaders prepared the Communion service, which (if I heard him correctly) consisted of three packages of crackers and three Cokes. The first three persons to take part in Communion ate and drank all of it. Nothing was left for anyone else. The elder's question: Was any sin committed?

A good discussion ensued, some of which I couldn't follow, so I can't report whether the consensus found the three guilty of sin or not. Certainly they were guilty of discourtesy. They failed to "discern the body" of Christ, not fully realizing they are a part of a larger whole.

The late novelist Flannery O'Connor, a serious Roman Catholic believer, wrote a friend who was becoming a member of the church. Miss O'Connor wanted to "do something celebrative" for the occasion. Her solution was to go

> to Communion for you and your intention Easter morning, and since we will then share the same actual food, you will know that your being where you are increases me and the other way around.[5]

Don't you like her word *increases* here? This is what happens to us when we approach the Lord's Table in thanksgiving for him and for our fellow communers. We are increased by his and their presences.

Another helpful insight is offered by Eugene Peterson, who claims

> the eucharistic meal maintains the social shape of salvation. Eating together is an act of trust and love among friends and strangers, an accepted invitation to equality with one another before God. We do not customarily, or if we can help it, eat alone. We come together with others, with family and friends. We demonstrate basic courtesies at the table. It is the place we learn consideration and forgiveness. It is also the place to which we invite strangers, hospitality being the means by which we bridge suspicion and loneliness, gathering the outsider into the place of nurture and acceptance.[6]

So we give thanks for the rich social and spiritual lives we enjoy because One took bread and cup and blessed and gave.

Have I made Communion sound enough like celebration? I hope so. I tend to become too serious on this subject, because the churches I have attended make a practice of dimming the lights, playing soft organ music in the background, and demanding absolute quiet of the congregation. Often attention is called to Communion as funeral service; we are remembering our crucified Lord.

I have no quarrel with this approach. We all need a little quiet time in our lives. It is good to be still and know that he is God.

There's one more word to be said, however, and that is that we are remembering, recommitting ourselves to, and giving thanks for, a Person and persons we love. In healthy love relationships, there is a large element of merriment and celebration. Even funeral services are sometimes punctuated with laughter, especially so when the deceased was deeply loved and is fondly remembered. What Abraham Maslow says in another context, in which he discusses healthy people's love and sex lives, applies here. He compares it to "the games of children and puppies. It is cheerful, humorous, and playful."[7]

Ari Goldman's reminiscences of his Jewish childhood capture the essence of communal thanksgiving. He describes the Sabbath morning congregation descending from synagogue prayers to the social hall, the standing and chatting around the tables until the rabbi says the *b'racha,* the blessing, on the wine so that everyone can begin. Goldman grew up with these b'rachas, an essential part of the everyday life of an Orthodox youngster.

"Baruch atah Adonai Eloheynu Melech Ha'olam hamotzi lechem min ha'aretz," one says before eating bread. "Blessed are you, God, King of the Universe, who brings forth bread from the ground." There is another b'racha for

189

vegetables (". . . who brings forth the produce of the ground") and another for pastries (". . . who created different kinds of cakes"). And then there is a whole different category—b'rachas that you say when you see lightning or a rainbow, b'rachas after recovering from an illness and, most routinely, a long laundry list of b'rachas in the daily prayers—giving thanks for waking up, for freedom, for new clothes, for the ability to study Torah—there is even one, recited by boys and men, thanking God for not making us women, and another, recited by males and females, praising God for not making us Gentiles. Upon leaving the bathroom, we make a b'racha thanking God for our internal plumbing system. In yeshiva, our rebbe taught us that "a good Jew" has to say one hundred b'rachas a day.

Goldman's mother was diligent on b'racha patrol. Nothing could pass young Ari's lips without thanks. "After she gave me a cookie, she would watch closely for the mumble." As a result, the habit of saying b'rachas never left him. He says it sometimes looks as if he is talking to his food before popping it in his mouth. "It is an involuntary act and, on those rare occasions when I think about what it is that I'm doing, I kind of like it. In the great scheme of things, it seems only right to give thanks."[8]

How can anyone complain, then, that regular, weekly Communion is too frequent? Is it too much to offer formal thanks once a week? Regular celebrants at the Lord's Table find the practice of giving thanks habit forming, until we find ourselves like Ari Goldman, unconsciously mumbling thanks. G. K. Chesterton has caught the spirit:

You say grace before meals. All right. But I say grace before the concert and the opera, and grace before the play and pantomime, and grace before I open a book, and grace before sketching, painting, swimming, fencing, boxing, walking, playing, dancing and grace before I dip the pen in the ink.[9]

When one's whole being is grateful, every opportunity to say so is cherished.

Especially when surrounded by loved ones, as we are at the Lord's Table.

This is the reason we say we *celebrate* Communion.

[1]Donald Bridge and David Phypers, *Communion: The Meal that Unites?* Harold Shaw, 1981, pp. 71, 72, 74.

[2]*The Lord's Supper.* New York: Harper and Brothers, 1948, p. 32.

[3]M. Scott Peck, *What Return Can I Make?* New York: Simon and Schuster, 1985, pp. 100, 101.

[4]Robert Hicks, *Uneasy Manhood.* Nashville: Oliver Nelson, 1991, p. 157.

[5]*The Habit of Being, Letters of Flannery O'Connor,* ed. Sally Fitzgerald. New York: Vintage 1979, p. 150.

[6]*Reversed Thunder.* San Francisco: Harper and Row, 1988, p. 158.

[7]Abraham H. Maslow, *Motivation and Personality.* NY: Harper and Row, 1970, p. 195.

[8]Ari L. Goldman, *The Search for God at Harvard.* NY: Times Books, Random House, 1991, pp. 14, 15.

[9]G. K. Chesterton, quoted in *Christian Ministry,* July 1983.